ROBIN TRAYWICK WILLIAMS

BUSH HOGS

A•N•D

OTHER SWINE

Bush Hogs and Other Swine
1st Printing

Cataloging-in-publication data for this book is available from
The Library of Congress.
ISBN: 978-0-9827019-4-2

Robin Traywick Williams
Author

For information write:

Dementi Milestone Publishing, Inc.
Manakin-Sabot, VA 23103
Dementi@aol.com
www.dementimilestonepublishing.com

Cover design by Tucker Conley
tuckerriver@va.metrocast.net

Manuscript design by Jayne Hushen
jehushen@verizon.net
www.HushenDesign.com

Printed in the USA

Other books by Robin Traywick Williams
Chivalry, Thy Name is Bubba

With all my love to Cricket,
who has been the quintessential "husband to the rescue,"
playing a supportive Ricky Ricardo to my Lucy for more than 30 years

To Jeff,
a country boy
at heart —
Enjoy!
Robin Williams
12/9/10

Table of Contents

Foreword

by Earl Hamner

To be born poor in the backwoods of the Blue Ridge Mountains of Virginia during the height of the Great Depression would make it unlikely for a boy to venture far beyond the horizon. Yet, I have worked or lived in several of the world's great cities such as London, Paris, Tokyo, Sydney, Chicago, New York and my present home, Los Angeles.

I never really became a Londoner, or a Parisian, or a Chicagoan. When I lived in Paris, I would take a walk through the vast cemetery Pere Lachaise, and the image of that small family plot back in Nelson County would come to haunt me. Years later when I would come out of my office at Rockefeller Center in December and see that stunning Christmas tree, my mind would go to a modest little cedar, decorated with dime store baubles and homemade garlands, standing in a corner of my parents' home in Schuyler. Even today I may vote in California, but my roots are in Virginia, and Virginia will always be my home. Sometimes the urge to "go home" is so urgent that it is hard to keep from dashing off to the airport.

Most of us exiles share this same gravitational pull. Most recently I learned it from another Virginian, the writer Robin Traywick Williams.

Robin was living in Hawaii, working on a novel and, as she described it, "having succumbed to the charming aimlessness of life in paradise."

She describes it best in her own words:

"One evening as I dressed for dinner in the tropics amid the cloying scent of plumeria and ginger, the sounds of night in Virginia suddenly enveloped me. Homesickness for Virginia hammered me like the

Bermuda High in July. I could feel the humidity and smell the cedar trees and hear the red tailed hawks. Within days, I made plans to go home, finish school and NEVER leave Virginia again."

Hawaii's loss was Virginia's gain, for Robin did give in to that urgent need to go home. Since then she has enriched Virginia life in the political arena, as an author, a columnist and notably in her efforts to provide for the health and humane treatment of racehorses.

I am personally grateful to Robin Williams for proving a point. I have long contended that rural America, and most certainly rural Virginia, is the repository of so many of those qualities that are achingly absent in many of our social encounters in cities. Robin confirms this in her writing.

There are just terribly many of us in cities. We compete not just for a way to make a living but also for living space, for air to breathe, for courtesy, grace and dignity. And sadly we come up lacking in each of these areas. We become surly and cranky and forget the good manners we were taught as youngsters growing up in Virginia.

In her writing Robin celebrates the individualism and self-reliance of rural Virginia folks. She loves country life and its old-fashioned values. She reveres the natural world, the beauty that surrounds her there in central Virginia, and she writes of it with radiance.

Robin is above all humorous. In this book she writes an amusing account of the family cat that "took to her bed after receiving B-12 injections." There are the awful circumstances that led her to request a lawn mower for her birthday. And my favorite event is the one in which she describes "a family reunion attended by four hundred people some of whom didn't even know each other!"

This is hilarious stuff. Don't take my word for it. Give yourself a treat. Go buy a copy of "Bush Hogs and Other Swine" and be prepared to laugh out loud!

August 2010

Earl Hamner, recognized novelist, screenwriter, television writer, and voice over recording artist, has roots which run deep in Virginia's Blue Ridge Mountains.

In the early 1900s, the Hamner family moved from its James River tobacco farm to the town of Schuyler on the eastern slope of the Blue Ridge. That homesite became the basis for his book released in 1970, The Homecoming, which was published by Random House. It became a CBS Christmas television special, and then in 1972, the basis for the long-running series, The Waltons. The first year it received five Emmys, and it ran for nine years.

Today, Earl Hamner still writes every day and is still involved in television, although he claims that on his visits to the networks they offer him a glass of warm milk and help him to his seat! If anything, he has stepped up his book writing. Goodnight John-Boy (2002), The Twilight Zone Scripts of Earl Hamner (2003), and Generous Women (2006) have ensued.

Earl Hamner summed up the credo of his life and work to the electronic media students at the University of Cincinnati:

"Without courage, honor, compassion, pity, love and sacrifice, as William Faulkner pointed out, we know not of love, but lust. We debase our audience. But we can ennoble and enrich our viewers and ourselves in our journey through this good time, this precious time, this great and wonderful experience we call life."

CHAPTER 1

Monkeying with the Mower

You know that period in April when the grass shoots up on a Monday and you can't get it mowed until Saturday and you fret about the place looking abandoned? In our case, it's more like the grass shoots up on Monday and we can't get it mowed until June.

This is because my husband, Cricket, insists on cutting the grass himself with his antique mower.

Cricket jealously guards his monopoly on mowing because protecting the delicate health of his pre-historic mower is easier, apparently, than brow-beating a child to cut the grass. The riding mower is an 18 hp Craftsman that he got from Sears Roebuck right after we got married 25 years ago. About 10 years ago, Cricket and Worth Higgins began bragging about the longevity of their respective riding mowers, and ever since, Cricket has been determined to outdo Worth in the Oldest Living Lawn Mower contest.

Actually, I think Worth conceded the field to Cricket five or six years ago, but Cricket is a man obsessed. For some time now, I've been begging him to retire the Craftsman to the Lawn Mower Hall of Fame and get one of those fancy new jobs with a five-foot-wide mowing deck and two handles that make it spin around on a dime. He doesn't deign to respond.

One day I was at my friend Buck Fevre's house, lamenting the overgrown state of our farmette. "Cricket is the bottleneck. He's the only one who can make the mower run, so nobody else can cut the grass," I said gloomily.

One of Buck's boys overheard my remark and said, "Nobody can cut the grass but the dad? That's great!"

I guess it's all in your perspective.

Every spring, Cricket spends the first nice Saturday "working on the mower." I have no idea what that means, from a technical standpoint. I do know it means several trips to the hardware store and a phone call to Sears to order a new belt, followed by a week's delay until the belt comes in. Depending on how things go, he usually gets to mow before the grass gets much over knee-high.

But this year there were complications.

It rained several Saturdays. Then Cricket went out of town on a couple of weekends. When he got around to "working on the mower," the grass was already shoulder high. He made mysterious noises in the garage all day while I burrowed a tunnel out to the mailbox. Finally, I heard the engine catch and Cricket rode triumphantly out of the garage and began mowing the front yard. After a few minutes, though, the engine shut off. Cricket came and got me and directed me to sit on the mower and steer while he pulled it back to the garage with the pickup truck.

"Belt," he said.

He got the spare belt installed in a short time and again I heard the engine running – just long enough to get as far away as possible from the garage. We did the pickup truck pull again, but now he had run out of belts. And he had to figure out what was eating up the belts. So he got the tractor and lifted the front of the mower up with the front-end loader. He removed the clutch assembly and called Sears to order a replacement part. They told him demand for clutch assemblies for 25-year-old lawn mowers was low and they had discontinued the part. So then he took the worn part to a welding shop and rejuvenated it somehow. But then the conventional belt didn't fit. So then he drove around to every auto parts store in town, buying belts of various sizes.

As the weeks passed without a haircut, the yard went from unkempt to scraggly to scary. The chickweed looked like kudzu and the dandelions were starting to look like sunflowers. The National Zoo called and asked if they could fence it for monkey habitat. The Brazilian government called to ask if we would maintain it as replacement acreage for the rain forest.

I got so desperate I asked for a lawn mower for my birthday. My friend, Alton Payne, who helps around the place, was enormously amused at the idea. After he got through guffawing, he said, “You don’t want a lawn mower for your birthday. Get Cricket to give you a diamond.”

Now there’s a thought.

“What am I going to do with a diamond?” I asked Alton.

“Wear it out,” he said. “Wear it out and show your friends.”

Not that he needed any additional incentive, but Cricket, when I told him what Alton suggested, redoubled his efforts to get a belt on the mower. Just recently, as I lay in the hammock, listening to the monkeys chattering in the jungle, I heard the encouraging sound of the mower’s engine roaring to life.

CHAPTER 2

Today's Wildlife Adventure...

Today's wildlife adventure involved a fledgling wren who, on one of his very first flights, flew through the terrace doors into the clutches of Buttons the cat. This occurred the day after I extracted a skink from Buttons' mouth and put it outside. *That* occurred the day after Buttons brought a chipmunk into the house.

I don't understand why chipmunks aren't extinct. They are so dumb. They must be like rabbits and have a million babies. The cats catch them all the time. I've saved many a one and locked the cats in the house awhile to give it a chance to catch its breath and run away – only to turn the cats out an hour later and have them catch the same one again. What they (the chipmunks) do is run *around* the tree. They have perfectly good climbing skills, just like squirrels, but when a cat starts chasing them, they forget how to climb. Even the dog can catch chipmunks.

So the chipmunk in the house got away from Buttons and – being the Albert Einstein of chipmunks – he climbed up the living room curtains.

The first thing you have to do when you are herding wild animals in the house is collect the cats and shut them up in the laundry room, because cats do not have the right instinct for herding. Another thing you have to do is remove all the valuable fragile stuff that might get broken in the melee that herding wild animals inevitably turns into.

With the cats and the bric-a-brac out of the way, next you position your assistant, armed with a broom, in the hallway leading to the rest of the house.

When I began herding this chipmunk, he proved unfamiliar with the process. His response to my broom was to run back and forth along the curtain rod several times with his tail stuck up in the air, causing me to laugh at the ridiculousness of the whole scene. Eventually he made a spectacular dive and raced past the wide open door to the outdoors and towards the hall, where my able assistant made a brilliant save, turning him back with deft broom-handling.

Unfortunately, despite our herding skill, Albert Einstein ended up behind the piano.

Plan B, then, was to pull one end of the piano out from the wall and build a chute to the door with throw pillows. The drawback to Plan B is, you never know when the chipmunk is gone, so you have to leave the door open for the rest of the day.

My husband, Cricket, says we could avoid a lot of these problems if I would keep the doors closed, but, after a long winter, I love to open the house to the breezes and bird songs of spring. Plus, a lot of times I need to air out the house after I burn up something on the stove.

It's sort of a catch-22 to say I was airing out the house when the wren flew in. I heard a commotion and looked up to see Buttons leaping and snatching at the tail feathers of a baby wren who was learning to fly.

They say the sight of the gallows focuses the mind wonderfully. As his parents called helpful instructions from the spruce tree outside – *Flap your wings!* – the little wren focused for all he was worth on learning to fly. *Flap flap. Flap flap flap.*

Meanwhile, I grabbed Buttons and shut her in the laundry room. As the wren hid behind a houseplant and caught his breath, I picked up my animal-herding broom. After a spell, the fledgling, older and wiser now, flew home to momma.

Buttons is, of course, massively frustrated by my interference in her hunting. But I have to try to save the birds because I feel guilty about feeding them and drawing them to our house when we have four healthy and extremely carnivorous cats. As for the chipmunks and skinks, mainly I don't want them tortured or chased inside the house.

My family has refrained from pointing out the inconsistency in my rescuing wild animals from the cats while at the same time leaning out the back door with the .22 and blasting squirrels off the bird feeder. The cats undoubtedly think there's a double standard here, too. *Oh, <u>you</u> can* *hunt all the squirrels you want, but we can't catch so much as one itsy-bitsy lizard. It's not fair.*

You're right, cat. Life is not fair.

Editorial comment from Katie Bo: Only in the Williams' family do you drive past your mother in the driveway and she calls out, "Leave the door open. There's a chipmunk in the piano. Love you. Bye." Then you have to drive around the dead squirrel she shot in the driveway. Then you go in and there's a pan burning on the stove.

Author's note: A skink is a small common lizard with an electric blue stripe down its back. When this column originally appeared in the paper, someone unfamiliar with skinks had helpfully corrected what she thought was a typo, changing the word in the opening paragraph to read "skunk."

CHAPTER 3

Cable News

One of the best things about having a teenager in the house is that you have at least a tangential exposure to pop culture. Thanks to Katie, I now know about Jude Law. Admittedly, for a long time I thought "Jude Law" was a hot new cop show, but recently I learned that Jude Law is a hot new actor. Some magazine dubbed him the sexiest man alive. (What happened to Brad Pitt? Johnny Depp?)

You never know when knowledge like that is going to come in handy.

YEAH ... EXCEPT I THINK JUDE LAW IS THE BIGGEST OBNOXIOUS PERSON IN THE WORLD!!!

(Please pardon the interruption by the teenager who edits my column and keeps me updated on pop culture.)

Being in possession of one pop culture factoid can often save you from exposure as a closet nerd.

EVEN IF SHE POSSESSED TWO POP CULTURE FACTOIDS, IT WOULDN'T BE ENOUGH TO PROTECT HER.

Before I had Katie, I used to rely on my mother, whose knowledge of pop culture, while occasionally skewed, is definitely more encompassing than mine. To illustrate this, my brother Cris likes to tell about the time he and Momma were talking about rock bands, and Momma made a reference to "KISS."

"What," I asked innocently, "is KISS?"

Later in life I actually interviewed lead singer Gene Simmons and met all the KISS band members, who were all rigged out in their black and white face paint, tight pants and platform shoes, but that day with Momma and Cris, I was clueless.

"Oh, Rob-in!" Momma exclaimed.

"Too much PBS," my brother averred.

Recently, I had lunch with six or eight of my women friends, and the conversation was lively, hilarious and, to me, astonishing. The women were mostly in their 40s, most with children and most with jobs – a couple with serious careers. The talk turned to the news of a 57-year-old woman who had given birth to twins. Everyone was aghast at the notion of being pregnant at that age and even more aghast at the notion of having a teenager – excuse me, two teenagers -- when she was 70.

"And they're not even biologically related to her!"

In short order, my luncheon companions named two other elderly women having babies: Christie somebody and Joan Lundin.

Intimate details of the pregnancies flew back and forth across the table like dinner rolls at a food fight. There was discussion of whose eggs were impregnated by whose sperm and whether delivery was natural or by Caesarian section.

"No, she had a donor egg but they used her husband's sperm."

"They implanted four embryos but only one took."

"She had a girl. Five weeks early but the baby weighed seven pounds, six ounces."

"Imagine if she'd carried it to term!"

"Imagine trying to lose all that weight at her age."

They segued naturally into weight loss.

"Oprah lost 487 pounds again."

"Did she lose it or did she have her stomach stapled?"

"No, she lost it."

"Well, it was pretty fast. Two weeks or so."

"Gene had his stomach stapled and it still took a month to lose 93 pounds."

"This is the third time. It's hard on your body to do all that ping-ponging."

"She used the Celebrity Person's Magic diet."

I had nothing to contribute to the deranged-old-lady-has-baby discussion, but I do know, personally, a celebrity who has had his stomach stapled (not Jude Law). However, before I could leap in with my impressive factoid, the ladies were comparing the restrictions of the Atkins and South Beach diets, and the moment was lost.

I listened to this lively exchange for about 20 minutes, amazed that everybody at the table seemed to know, in great detail, all about the reproductive and gastronomic lives of people they had never met. This led me to wonder: Why was I so far out of the mainstream that I didn't know these things? Where did these busy women find time to acquire this vast store of knowledge? How did I get on this planet?

Finally, during a brief pause, I gasped, "How…how do you know all this stuff?"

"Oh!" they laughed in unison. "You don't have cable!"

There. I was exposed. A nerd living in a substandard, hick home without such basic amenities as 275 television channels. How could I show my face in this company again? Recovering quickly, I said, "But you don't need cable to watch PBS."

Not good enough, I could tell. I had to prove that I, too, had a (limited) store of useless information about vacuous people whose lives would never (I hoped) intersect mine. I tried again. "Did you know KISS wrote the theme music for 'Jude Law'?"

SHE IS NOT MY MOTHER!!!! WE ARE NOT BIOLOGICALLY RELATED!!!

CHAPTER 4

Can You Wear Leder Hosen with a Muu-muu?

There's an old line comparing men to sofas: They might look great in the store, but when you get them home, they don't always go with the rest of your décor. That may or may not be true of men, but it describes in stunning understatement any item purchased while on vacation.

We recently went to New York for a three-day vacation and bought a chicken. We had not gone to New York with such a purchase in mind, but that is what happens when you go on vacation. You shop. And you buy things you don't need, can't use, can't afford and, with amazing frequency, don't even like.

You relax with the adult beverage of your choice – which often turns out to be something you've never chosen before and which, you swear, if God lets you live, you will never never never even think of ordering again and whose existence will become a powerful hyperbolic reference for you for the rest of your life: "I'd drink a Goldslager Rusty Nail again before I'd let our daughter go to a coed sleep-over with a guy, especially *that* guy!"

After a few days of such relaxation, you sink comfortably into the culture and you start to think, *This is such a cool place. Why don't we have a herd of ceramic elephants back home? Why don't we sit on the floor and eat with chop sticks?*

Pretty soon you find yourself watching Polynesian dancers with a discriminating eye and imagining that, with the right brightly-colored muu-muu, you could produce the same effect. Or you find yourself seriously contemplating a $525 porcelain kitten less than one inch high suitable for the figurine collection that you, alas, don't have but that you could begin, today, with this very purchase.

That's the thing about getting away for a rejuvenating break. You become rejuvenated to about age 10 in your thinking. You go on vacation, you happily embrace the local culture, and before you know it, you've bought a sombrero with a five-foot wingspan that you are, at the moment you hand over your money, planning to wear…where?

Too late. You've signed the Visa chit and that cultural artifact is yours. Now all you have to do is figure out how to get it home. Sombreros do not fold. Neither do concrete Mexicans.

Nor do, say, larger-than-life metal reproductions of gamecocks engaged in a fight to the death. When my mother bought the latter on an economic trade mission to Tijuana with Gov. George Allen, she and I spent most of the next day traipsing around San Diego, trying to get the irascible roosters in a box. Shipping was so prohibitive that Momma briefly considered buying an airplane ticket for her prized fowl. I don't know how she finally got them back to Virginia, but she was determined enough to keep them that she looked into renting an apartment and moving to San Diego.

As you fly home with your purchase, you begin to imagine incorporating into your wardrobe *leder hosen* or decorating the TV room with an end table made of an elephant's foot. Next, you begin thinking up reasons to tell your family why you bought this treasure. By the time you land, you are wondering whether to donate it to the fundraiser at school or the silent auction at your club.

If I'd played my cards right in New York, I could have had a Persian rug instead of a chicken. So seductive is vacation shopping that even my sensible husband relaxed on a visit to a furniture store in SoHo. He was fingering the rugs, asking how many knots per inch, analyzing patterns. I was amazed at the prospect of his spending that kind of money on a spur-of-the-moment purchase.

But I couldn't get the chicken out of my mind. It was a *less* than life-sized model rooster in authentic gamecock plumage. So I nixed the rug and held out for a $28 New York chicken.

And I was happy when I got it home and found the perfect spot for it: on the mantle next to the stuffed fox. You know, predator and prey. It was, I was sure, the only successful vacation purchase ever made and I was proud of it.

But last week my 10-year-old cousin Tray, a die-hard Clemson tiger fan, fussed at me for displaying the mascot of his arch-rival, the South Carolina gamecocks.

So, I guess it's off to the school auction.

CHAPTER 5

Kitchen Gadgets: a Burning Issue

We had dinner with some friends recently at their house. The wife made a fabulous meal which, even without the urbane conversation as a *lagniappe*, would have been enough for us to proclaim this one of the most delightful evenings ever.

Since the butler, the chef and the scullery maid were all on vacation in the south of France, I helped her in the kitchen afterwards. And I was amazed at the number and diversity of kitchen devices she had used to prepare dinner. There were, in fact, so many gadgets flecked with carrot curls and appliances drooling raspberry sauce that there was no place on the counter to stack the dirty dishes. (In our house, we would just put them on the floor for the dog to lick while we made room on the counter, but this wasn't that kind of house.)

It's amazing how many people cook like that.

Once, in a similar situation, we saw the hostess stack the electric frying pan on the toaster oven, pile up the pans and lids on the stove and get out an electric grinder the size and shape of a box of salt. Then she put a handful of coffee beans in the top and ground them into dust. Then she got out the percolator and performed that ceremony with the paper doilies, the coffee grounds and the sacred water that people who are serious about their coffee do. Then she got out a giant electric mixer with a set of nested bowls and more attachments than my husband, Cricket, has for his hand drill. After selecting the right tool and attaching it, she pureed some apricots. Then, switching bowls and attachments, she whipped some cream. Finally, she assembled the dessert, beginning with ice cream dipped with a special dipper that she had warmed in the microwave and ending with white chocolate curls extruded from an electric chocolate-curl extruder.

I'll bet if the power went out they'd starve to death. (Of course, they probably have a generator.)

Anyway, I am truly awed by such mechanical abundance.

I'm pretty much a minimalist when it comes to kitchen gadgets. The most complicated tool that I have is a knife. My limited collection of kitchen tools may be due to the fact that my cooking skills are limited to recipes perfected in the days before electricity was invented.

I can make my entire repertoire with a big spoon, a sharp knife and a fork. Occasionally, I use all three. To wit: Use the knife to cut up a chicken (assuming someone else has already decapitated and plucked it); use the spoon to scoop a big glob of bacon grease into the pan; use the fork to turn the frying chicken pieces over in the hot grease.

What else could you possibly need? My dinner guests might say, Well, you use a cast iron frying pan, but I say, That's not a gadget, that's a basic tool no proper kitchen would be without.

The truth is I couldn't stand to wash all those gadgets. If the dog could lick the coffee grinder or the chocolate-curl extruder clean, that would be one thing, but scrub all those little grooves and holes clean? The time you save in preparation on the front end you lose cleaning up on the back end. Plus, you probably have to have a specialized chocolate-curl extruder cleaner to get all the crumbs out. Where would it end?

Cricket would be wary of any attempt on my part to incorporate gadgets into my cooking routine. He doesn't think I've mastered to ones we already have.

Take the stove. Cricket is confident in my ability to turn it on and cook something in a pan. What he is less confident about is my ability to turn it off before the stuff in the pan burns. His lack of confidence is well-placed. At least once a week, I leave something on the stove to burn, usually the rice. Last week I burned some squash while I was standing next to it. I was slicing tomatoes and suddenly detected an intense, sort of grilled-squash odor.

Which leads me to confess that there is a power tool without which I cannot operate my kitchen: a cell phone. I have Nancy Jewell's number programmed for speed dial so that when I go in town and realize that I left a pan of snaps on the stove two hours earlier, I can call and ask her to run over to the house and turn the stove off.

If the house isn't on fire.

CHAPTER 6

Forces of Nature 1, Bureaucracy 0

It's pretty hard to watch days of television coverage of the aftermath of Katrina showing an endless archipelago of rooftops or refugees clustered on a highway overpass or miles of white beaches decorated with third-world thatch-turned-kindling wood and not feel angry that this is happening in the United States. We are the richest, most advanced nation in the world. We've put men on the moon and brought them home safely, for goodness' sake, why we can't we pluck a few people off rooftops? We've sent sophisticated sensors to pinpointed locations light-years from Earth, so why can't we deliver a few kegs of water to refugees in Louisiana?

Ours is the disbelief of the scientist who suddenly discovers the dinosaurs in Jurassic Park have replicated on their own. The power of Nature is truly humbling – the Christmas tsunami, Mt. St. Helen's eruption, the San Francisco earthquake of 1989 – and Nature delivered one of its most humbling messages to the Gulf Coast last month.

But many Americans are in denial. They see the U. S. government as the solution to all problems, including warding off bad weather. For instance, no one here was angry about the tsunami because, after all, that occurred in a place with a far less advanced government than ours. It was unthinkable that something like that could happen here, or, if it did, that the government wouldn't fix everything up in a day or two.

Let's get real. No matter who the President is, government at its best is still a bureaucratic behemoth steeped in molasses, shackled by rules dictating behavior for pre-set situations. One of those rules is that the federal government can't come in until the state asks for help. Although the President had declared a federal disaster *before* the hurricane and begged the Louisiana governor to permit an expedited federal response, the governor waffled, leaving government officials dutifully focused on getting the paperwork signed in triplicate before relief efforts could begin.

Meanwhile, the catastrophe itself was reaching epic proportions.

Remember how unbelievable it was so see the World Trade Towers reduced to rubble in just a few minutes, crushing and incinerating 3,000 innocent people at the same time? That event, still difficult to grasp, was physically confined to two city blocks. The devastation of Katrina – just as messy, much more toxic, lethality still unknown – covers an area the size of Great Britain. It also affects 1,000,000 people in three states who have lost their homes, their jobs, all their possessions and, in many cases, loved ones, pets, cars and the wherewithal to rebuild their lives.

Remember, too, that the flood waters of New Orleans have no way to recede naturally, given that the city exists in the basement of the state. When hurricane Gaston flooded Richmond last year, the water eventually drained into the James River. New Orleans will remain under six-eight-ten feet of water until pumps can shift the stinking soup uphill to Lake Pontchartrain.

Complaints about the Department of Homeland Security are misplaced. There is a huge difference between homeland security and disaster response. Homeland security involves forestalling attacks and protecting vulnerable points in the nation's infrastructure. Disaster response involves rapid deployment of manpower and supplies under difficult conditions; search and rescue; and expeditious repair of basic infrastructure to facilitate the above activities. Disaster response is a sign that homeland security has somehow failed.

If you want to improve the immediate response to a catastrophe, you need to separate disaster response from homeland security and turn it over to the military, or to an agency constituted on the military model. Ideally, this outfit would have the ability to coordinate inter-governmental response. The bureaucratic model is inadequate to deal with disaster response. The last thing thirsty victims need is a bottle of water wrapped in red tape.

The inevitable Katrina Report will say some units of government performed splendidly (mostly the military outfits) and some rightfully earned the scorn of the country (*inter alia*, New Orleans police officers who hid neither their badges nor their faces while looting a Wal-Mart; the New Orleans mayor and Louisiana governor, who failed to evacuate or otherwise protect the state's most vulnerable citizens in the state's most vulnerable locale; Louisiana officials who for years failed to focus available dollars on New Orleans' notoriously fragile levee system).

Despite the initial, depressing images, recovery efforts were in high gear by week's end. We are, after all, a can-do people with massive resources at our disposal. The wealth and resiliency of America remains an awesome thing to contemplate, thanks to the great engine of free enterprise. What other country could absorb – without collapsing, with scarcely a ripple of discomfort to most citizens – this massive hit on its economy? It will be messy and painful and costly and the progress will be uneven, but do you have any doubt in your mind that the cities and towns along the Gulf Coast will be rebuilt?

There will be winners and losers. Some will never regain what they lost. Some will, as Barbara Bush suggested, end up in better circumstances. Some alert individuals will take advantage of opportunities for upward mobility that never would have occurred in their antediluvian world.

We would be well-advised to take this as a lesson in the limitations of government and the value of self-reliance. So: pay your taxes, but pack your own lifeboat. And don't forget the dog crate.

CHAPTER 7

The Wars of Hoses

Weather is definitely a local thing. Notice how large portions of the land along the Gulf of Mexico have been swept away by Hurricanes Katrina and Rita (and, perhaps by press time, some other cyclone as well), whereas large portions of Virginia have shriveled up like a slug with salt on it? Hurricane Ophelia bumped along the Carolinas for most of the month, dumping more water than the Amazon River, but all the while here in 23039 we remain drier than a vodka martini.

According to the media and the tree-huggers, hurricanes are caused by Republican presidents. But that's illogical, because the states that are most affected by hurricanes are all "red" states. Republican presidents would not smite their own. If Republican presidents caused hurricanes, you'd see them destroying places like Boston and New York City. So, clearly, hurricanes are caused by the Clintons.

The media and the tree-huggers also blame droughts on Republican presidents, which, again, is illogical. Droughts in Virginia are related to the Bermuda High, a weather phenomenon that arises over a mysterious area of the Atlantic Ocean notorious for gobbling up airplanes without a trace. Clearly, then, droughts are caused by the greedy capitalist points of the Bermuda Triangle: Boeing, Lockheed-Martin and Jenn-Aire.

When we had three or four years of drought around the turn of the century, it got so bad people's wells started drying up. Ours, which was never Niagara Falls to begin with, became even stingier and we feared a complete shut down. We had always had enough water to get by, as long as we didn't try to do too many water-intensive chores at the same time.

You couldn't fill up the water trough and then go take a shower, or run the clothes washer and the dishwasher at the same time. It amazes me now that I used some of our meager flow to water bushes, but I wrestled hoses around the yard endlessly during those dry years.

I'm happy to report that this dry spell has been much less painful than any I've ever endured. The hose situation is better, and so is the water situation.

As I have noted before, God never invented a more cunning instrument of torture than the garden hose. They're heavy, they're never long enough, and they always have a kink somewhere that cuts off the water. You can't hook them together because the ends are always in the driveway where they get run over by a car and bent.

I'm writing now to share with you my triumphant discovery: Cheap hoses are better. The expensive, heavy-duty hoses are just that, heavy. Unless you are in training for the Olympic wrestling team, you don't need to drag 300 pounds of hoses around the yard. I recently bought an inexpensive, lightweight hose, and it has been heavenly! I can whip it around like a sash, give it a snap when it hooks on a flagstone and coil it up like a belt. True, it's only fifty feet long, but I've decided anything beyond that range will just have to put down a deeper tap root.

I long to be like Jerri Marx. Recently I was talking to her about the trials of keeping things watered during a drought, moving hoses from bush to bush every hour, coiling muddy hoses on reels. Finally, I paused for her to make some sympathetic remark of shared suffering and she said, "I just don't water at all."

Now there's a liberating thought.

Our family made it through the three-year drought without losing our well, but even after the rains and hurricanes came, it seemed we were short of water all the time. So my husband, Cricket, decided to dig a second well. He retained Willie Swift and instructed him to dig until he reached "a lot" of water. One day during the well-drilling process, Willie came to the door to announce that he had hit "a lot" of water. I was thrilled. How much, I wanted to know, is "a lot"?

Well, he said, about 4,000 gallons a day.

That certainly sounded impressive, but I needed to have him put that in context. How much did we have before, with the old well?

Oh, about 300 gallons a day, he said.

So, I mused, for twenty-some years we lived in this house and bathed, washed clothes, raised a baby, watered a small herd of horses, grew vegetables and watered bushes with 300 gallons a day, but now – (At this point, our daughter went out the door and drove off to school.) – now that we have a teenaged girl in the house, we need 4,000 gallons a day.

And that's probably not enough.

CHAPTER 8

The Genealogy of Country Dogs

Kay Higgins used to have a wonderful brown dog named Lucy who, I'm sure, had a whole raft of aristocratic ancestors. It was apparent, however, that none of them were of the same breed, something that only enhanced Lucy's charm in Kay's opinion.

One time Kay and I were walking Lucy, and we met up with a neighbor. After exchanging pleasantries, the neighbor looked down her nose at Lucy and said, "Is she…any particular breed?"

Kay blushed for her beloved dog, and I blurted out, "She's a Nepalese goat dog."

The neighbor couldn't bring herself to admit she was unfamiliar with this rare and undoubtedly expensive breed, so she smiled, arched her eyebrows in approval and said, "Oh."

What I should have said was that Lucy was part of an ancient and hallowed class of dogs. Lucy was a country dog.

There are two breeds of country dog: The Lab-x and the cur dog, sometimes called a collie dog. They are distinguishable by their behavior as much as their conformation.

A cur dog is feisty, fast, barky and smallish. Cur dogs have either terrier or border collie blood, which contains amphetamine-loaded hemoglobin and accounts for their perpetual alertness. They are brown with long hair and curly tails. They make good watch dogs, in the sense of giving noisy, toothy warning to trespassers, and they have a tendency to kill cats and ground hogs.

Lab-xes come in two colors, black and black with a speck of white on the chest. A cross between a Labrador retriever and anything else, the

Lab-x has a short coat, a soulful expression and ears that hang down. Beyond that, the Lab-x is characterized by his tendency to sleep. Lab-xes make good boyhood companions, bed warmers, hearth rugs, dish lickers and Wal-Mart store greeters. They are especially useful as babysitters for rambunctious puppies and baby humans. They find killing cats to be far too much trouble. For a Lab-x, the height of his day is the seventeen seconds it takes for him to wolf down his supper.

Whereas cur dogs and Lab-xes share some traits, they differ in one important aspect. A cur dog is fiercely loyal to his owner, but a Lab-x will go off with anyone who offers him food.

This was brought home to me quite vividly recently. We always like to have a big dog because our land adjoins the State Farm, a.k.a., James River Correctional Center. One week there was a work crew, complete with shotgun-toting guard, clearing the fenceline we share with the Farm. As I was driving out one day, I saw Gyp, our Lab-x, trotting towards the inmates. I stopped and called to her, sending her back to the house. The guard assured me the dog wasn't bothering them. "She's been down here for lunch every day," he said cheerfully. "The men really like her."

How comforting. I guess we'll have to find a cur dog to counter the Wal-Mart greeter in the household.

Which begs the question, where do you get a country dog?

You certainly can't buy one. Country dogs come to you.

Ironically, some of the best country dogs are bred in town. The papered Saluki whelps a litter of mongrels and the embarrassed owner drives out to the country in the dark of night and drops the puppies off at the driveway of some nice farmer who, because he has lots of land for dogs, is presumed also to have lots of money for shots, neutering, de-fleaing, etc., of dogs.

That's how we got ours. Gyp is one of the rare yellow dog Lab-xes. She's so pale she's almost white, which is how we saw her that January night when someone dropped a 10-week-old puppy off at our driveway.

Despite her mysterious origins, Gyp has become a fine country dog. She is an excellent bed-warmer, doesn't bother the cats and licks the design off the dinner dishes. She is also an accomplished sleeper.

The other day I went out to the car and Gyp was sleeping in the driveway. She has finally figured out that I'm probably not going to take her anywhere, so she no longer gets up and approaches the car expectantly. That day she just lay there, flat on her side. I started the engine and noticed the noise did not stimulate Gyp to move. I saw that I could probably back up, turn around and drive away without running over her, but it would be close. So I eased back. She didn't move. Then I turned around. The dog slept on. So then I slowly drove away, detouring through the flowerbed on the left to avoid the dog.

As I looked in the rear-view mirror, Gyp twitched her shoulder to shake off a fly.

Note: As of press time, the two men who escaped from the State Farm on Saturday had not made any contact with Gyp, leading authorities to believe they had fled in the other direction.

CHAPTER 9

Take Me Home, Country Roads

The road is where country life impacts you first, often in the form of a deer leaping through your windshield. (Can we pass an ordinance against that?)

After such an initiation to rural life, you learn to note the places where deer like to cross the road, and you learn that when you see a doe run across the road, you need to slow down – because there are likely to be two or three more running along behind her.

For those used to city streets or interstate highways, driving on country roads is a whole 'nother experience. For one thing, the roads are surprisingly full of animals who take it as their right to use the paved byways. For another, the roads are full of people who are not in cars: walkers, joggers, cyclists, horseback riders and, of course, people who are just standing there talking. So you have to watch your speed.

Albert Payson Terhune, in his books about collies ("Lad: A Dog," et al.) used to complain bitterly about speeding motorists, to wit: "…a juggernaut careering down the highway at *forty-five* miles an hour." It sounds funny, but that's still pretty fast.

On a country road, a high-performance vehicle is one of George Taylor's tractors with a hay rake on the back. Nothing will teach you to stay on your side of a narrow, wind-y back road like meeting a giant tractor with a round baler on a blind curve. And nothing will teach you patience like following one.

After a good rain, the box turtles migrate across the pavement. When Katie Bo was little, we often stopped to rescue turtles from the road, and we frequently reported to Cricket on the number of turtles, waddling or squashed, that we had seen in the road: "One walking and two flats." Occasionally, we see a snapping turtle in the road. We don't try to rescue them, as they are generally ungrateful.

Snakes suffer the same ratio of survivability on the road as turtles, only instead of flat, they turn kinky. In the spring, when they come out of hibernation, and in the fall, when the nights get chilly, black snakes will warm themselves on the solar panels of pavement in the afternoon. I found one stretched across the driveway last week and had to leave the car a bit shy of the house to avoid disturbing him. (Question: Why don't snakes lie longways, so you can drive over them without chopping off their tails?)

As hard as we try to avoid hitting the nocturnal wildlife, there are inevitable casualties among the opossums, raccoons and foxes. Fortunately, there is an efficient carcass-removal unit in the country. The vultures work on a voluntary basis and motorists are urged to slow down in their work zones. Folks who have a romanticized vision of wildlife should take a good look at a vulture. They are some kind of ugly. I think even "Queer Eye for the Straight Guy" would take a pass on those dumpster-divers.

It's not always wildlife. You might see horses (usually with riders) or cattle (usually without riders) around any bend. Chickens and dogs can be found in or along many roads.

In fact, a good ol' country dog is perfectly at home on the road. Recently I wrote about the two breeds of country dog, cur dogs and Lab-xes. Some people pen up their hunting dogs, but a good country canine has the run of the place, from the front stoop to whatever boundary line he establishes as his own. For such dogs, the road is rather like the front porch.

Cur dogs busy themselves endlessly patrolling their property, ready to tag any stray cats or burglars who threaten their domain, boldly swaggering along the road to advertise their ferocity. Doona Ware is such a dog, city-born but country-raised. She runs herself thin, selflessly guarding the Ware homestead against myriad evil forces, often standing in the road to look both ways for trouble.

In contrast, Lab-xes feel that their mere appearance is a deterrent to would-be trespassers. Fortunately, this can be accomplished simply by sleeping in front of the house, sometimes in the road. No country dog understands this any better than Cordy Meyers. He moved here from the city but he clearly has the soul of an ol' country dog. Cordy wanders the neighborhood, following people away on their daily constitutional and then graciously accepting a ride home in their car. He has been known to take his post-prandial nap on the macadam in front of the Meyers' house, and of course the vehicles on the road just drive around him.

Dumb about traffic? No, just supremely confident that, in the country, the road is a shared by all.

CHAPTER 10

Deciphering the Menu in a Foreign Land

When you love and live in the country, there is always the danger that you will become so attached to the earth that you forget how to act when you go to town. Sometimes this means not knowing what to wear. Sometimes it means not knowing how to order in a restaurant.

I have always prided myself on disguising my country roots by dressing appropriately whenever I go to town. For years I carefully changed out of my country uniform – jeans – and put on a skirt, makeup, new hairdo, nail polish, pearls, etc., whenever I went in town to the grocery store, until I finally noticed that people wear jeans to the grocery store. In fact, people wear jeans everywhere, including weddings and the symphony, so it's getting to where dressing up to go to town is what makes you look like a hick.

Even if you get the clothes thing right, you will find there are other things that betray your rural roots, causing people to say you are "provincial," which, loosely translated, means "not knowing how to order coffee at Starbucks." That's because the real giveaway that you are from the country is when you are intimidated by the waiter at a restaurant. I'm not talking about La Petite France or the Four Seasons. I'm talking about the clerk at a franchise food establishment.

Going to a fast-food emporium is a daunting undertaking for the casual visitor. Obtaining nourishment there is like going to the doctor these days: you have to do a certain amount of self-diagnosis first and be prepared to rattle off what you want with some specificity. "I'll have an arterial bypass and a bilateral bunionectomy, to go, please. Can I have liposuction with that?"

Fast food places work hard to satisfy the impatient American psyche and to do this they have developed a system to turn your order into food almost instantly. But you, the customer, have an important part to play in making this system work. You must be decisive about your order and you must spit it out in the restaurant's unique vocabulary.

Well, I can do neither.

First of all, I am paralyzed by the number of choices. Even after I figure out, sort of, what I want to eat, I have a hard time identifying my choice on the menu board above the counter, so I have to ask a lot of questions. What is a Tonto burger? How do I know whether it's a better deal to get a double junior burger with medium fries and a small coke or to order the holiday special combo with super-sized drink and two sides (which I don't want)? And then some places automatically put pickles, mustard, catsup, strawberry jelly and tofu on every burger, and I'm not really a mustard-and-catsup-together person, so I have to ask about that.

If the burger comes with nothing on it, I have to ask for lettuce and tomato. Then the clerk asks me two or three times to repeat my order, until I figure out he doesn't know what a tomahto is.

And then there's the whole size thing. The menu board lists the available french fry sizes as "medium," "large," and "super duper." I usually want the smallest size, so I ask for "small fries." Nobody ever says, "We don't have small. You'll have to have medium." So I take that to mean when I say "small" I'm actually getting what they call "medium." But then what happens when I ask for "medium"? Do I get "medium" that is really their smallest size, or do I get "medium" that is their middle size, which they refer to as "large"? So I have to ask about that.

Meanwhile, the line behind me is growing longer.

When Katie Bo was young we often used the drive-through window. For one thing, the menu board there was more limited, and for another, I usually just ordered something for her. She always knew exactly what she wanted and fed me my lines, so that worked pretty well. (Now that she's 18, nothing has changed.)

But the drive-through window has some intimidating aspects of its own. Usually I can't hear the clerk very well and that leads to lots of hollering back and forth between me and the menu board. One time, when I was vainly trying to place our order by hollering at some faceless kiosk, Katie Bo pointed out that I was speaking to a newspaper box.

Sometimes dining out is more stress than I can bear and I just go home. After all, there's no dress code and I know the menu by heart.

CHAPTER 11

A Sleigh Full of Ponnies and Turquoise Kittens

I've always thought half the fun of giving a child an oh-wow present was building, making or wrapping it, as the case may be. Cricket has not always agreed with me on that, possibly because I usually have to call on him about 10:30 p.m. Christmas Eve to do something like attach 400 individual shingles to the roof of the new doll house.

I carried the idea too far at Easter one year. Katie Bo had begged the Easter Bunny for a rabbit every year, but he seemed to be impervious to her entreaties. One year I – he – fixed up a cat carrier as bunny habitat, put a stuffed rabbit inside and left her candy-filled Easter basket on top. That was a pretty disastrous year. First off, Whiskey the dog sneaked downstairs and ate all the hard-boiled eggs, shell and all, and threw up on the rug. Then, when Katie Bo saw the cat carrier she got so excited that she burst into tears when she found the fake bunny inside.

There are always unforeseen consequences when you bring an animal into the equation.

One year a pony came our way, and we had the opportunity to recreate the Christmas when Santa brought me a pony.

The difference was, I was nine and reasonably literate when Santa brought Jupiter, thus I had no trouble deciphering the note in my stocking. It was crudely printed with misspellings and horseshoes for some of the letters: Deer Robin, I am waiting for you at the barn. Come sone. Jupiter.

But Katie Bo was barely six when Santa Claus brought the aptly-named Surprise Package and she had to decipher a note in her stocking. Thanks to the excellence of Randolph Elementary School and the pedagogic skills of Mrs. Starke, Bo was well on her way to learning to read through the sensible method of phonics. We helped her decode Santa's note, which he had thoughtfully written in one-syllable words.

"...a good girl, so I left you a..."

Bo paused, then bravely tackled the next word, the verbal pot of gold.

"Puh-puh...ah-ah...nnn," she stuttered. Finally she looked at us quizzically. "Ponny?"

Somehow, when I remember the morning Jupiter arrived, I don't recall my parents' saying anything pedantic like, "The 'y' makes the 'o' long."

But it worked, and the next moment was the payoff for Cricket and me.

"A pony? A real live pony?" Bo leaped on the sofa and looked out the window at the barn.

"That's what it sounds like," we said, equally amazed at Santa's generosity.

"Well, I'm going yippying down to the barn," she announced.

Just the reaction that makes parents line up outside Must-Have Gizmos R Us at 3 a.m. in a blizzard to get their hands on the coveted toy-of-the-year.

One year our project was a little girl's dressing table. There were plenty of pretty, frilly ones on the market, but I wanted to personalize Bo's, so I bought a plain one, found a small wooden bench to go with it and set about painting them to match. The color I selected was turquoise, but it came out a bit too electric, so I tried to tone it down by sponging it with white paint and stenciling birds and ribbons on it. I worked on it nightly in the kitchen after Bo went to bed.

The project turned out just the way most of my artsy-craftsy projects turn out – way more complicated than originally planned. For some reason, the paint wouldn't dry, and every time Cricket and I picked up the table to put it away in the basement, we smeared the design. Finally, we left it down there and I worked on it there.

On Christmas Eve we were still messing, literally, with the wet-painted table, when Mrs. Santa (a.k.a. Marilyn Palmore) arrived with a black and white kitten I had impulsively rescued from the SPCA. We set up a bed and a water bowl in the corner of the basement and let the kitten romp around.

Christmas morning, we went downstairs to turn on the tree lights, haul the (wet) table upstairs, find the kitten, etc., while Bo waited impatiently at the top of the stairs. When we found the kitten, she had turquoise paint all over her tuxedo coat. There was nothing to do but – quick – have Santa's elf write a note explaining that the kitten had gotten loose in Santa's workshop.

Bo bought the story. Now in second grade, she could decipher the note in her stocking all by herself.

CHAPTER 12

Norman Rockwell and the Yeast Packet

I've decided buying yeast is the height of optimism.

The other day I opened the cupboard door and there, stuffed behind the cereal bowls, were two yellow packets labeled "Fleishmann's Rapid Rise Highly Active Yeast." Out of curiosity, I checked the expiration date. One packet was only three months out of date; the other was from 2004.

I am eternally buying packets of yeast in the expectation that I will spend a leisurely day creating warm loaves of delicious-smelling homemade bread. I persist in this fantasy even though I regularly find in my cupboard packages of yeast old enough to have been used in the War between the States.

Baking homemade bread is such an old-fashioned occupation that it brings to mind churning butter or doing laundry on a washboard. For most people, the term "making bread" refers to a cat kneading his claws on the bed.

When I was 20 and engaged to be married, I approached my mother in a panic one day. "Ma! I don't know anything about cooking or keeping house! What am I going to do?"

She immediately took the matter in hand, ushering me into the kitchen where she taught me how to make quick biscuits from scratch, the only homemaking skill I possessed when I walked down the aisle three weeks later.

She herself made wonderful loaves of homemade bread and pans of soft cinnamon rolls, but she must have known I'd never have time to make yeast bread.

Because, really, who does?

The practice of baking bread has gone with the wind because nobody has all day to spend cooking something you can buy in the grocery store for less than two dollars (unless you live in Richmond and snow has been forecast). Making bread is not brain surgery, but it does take time, patience, focus and staying in one place, so that pretty much lets me out.

Nevertheless, once in a blue moon, usually around Christmas, I set aside a day and, armed with a new packet of yeast, I make bread.

When you make light rolls or bread, you have to do things that you never have to do in the preparation of any other dish. That is because of the yeast.

Yeast is a fungus and used to come in wet, clay-like cakes about an inch square. Yeast cakes are pretty hard to find nowadays because scientists have magically transformed the fungus cells into a dry grainy substance that keeps better than the wet cakes. But you have to reconstitute dry yeast to get it to "work." This is a delicate process.

First you have to dissolve the yeast in warm water – not too hot or you'll kill it. Then you have to scald some milk to kill the enzymes that might otherwise kill the yeast. Then you have to cool the scalded milk so the heat won't kill the yeast. Then you have to add sugar to make the chemical reaction that causes the yeast to ferment. Then you add the hops.

No, wait. Wrong recipe.

After you've made a living mass of bread dough, you have to knead it. You make like the cat sharpening his claws, working the dough until it is smooth. You keep kneading until you have achieved a Zen-like state of serenity or your arms fall off, whichever comes first.

Then you "round up" the dough in a greased bowl and set it on the hearth or a warm radiator to rise. Periodically, you punch the cloud of dough down into a blob and let it rise again. Eventually, you roll and shape the dough into loaves or rolls or pinwheels or braided wreaths and brush it with butter or stuff it with cinnamon-sugar. Then you let it rise *again* before it's ready to bake.

At this point, I'm always half-way expecting the recipe to say, "Rub two sticks together…" but, to my relief, it turns out that bread dough will bake just fine in an electric oven.

Making bread is time-consuming but in a very satisfying way. You have to stay home to make bread. You can't be running in and out. You're not busy with the dough itself all day, but you have to be there to keep an eye on it and do something to it every so often. And you have to keep the kitchen warm so the dough will rise. What all this means is that you are there in a warm, sweet-smelling kitchen when your family comes home, and you can dust the flour off your hands, give them a hug and a kiss and fantasize about being the inspiration for Norman Rockwell's paintings.

Homemade bread is delicious, but making bread is really about slowing down to appreciate hearth and home and a loving family. Maybe that's why, no matter how busy I get, I keep buying yeast.

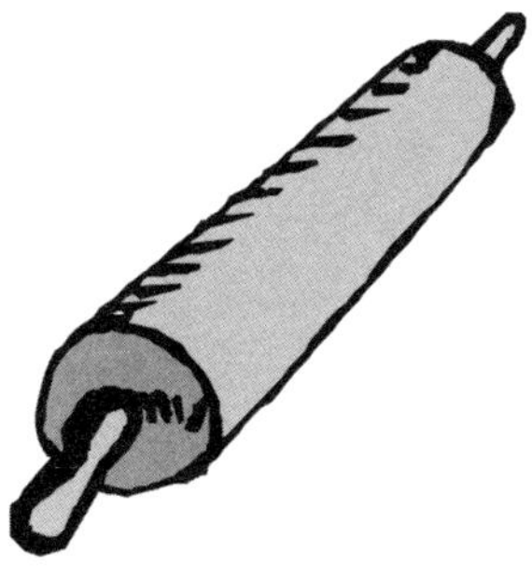

CHAPTER 13

Blessed Is the Bling

With the holidays drawing to a close, we are lying around bloated, sated and numbed by the month-long stimuli of redbluegreenorange chaser lights, last-second field goals, and commercials featuring remarkably dexterous animals. While we recover from a steady diet of whiskey-flavored, butter-injected, calorie-enhanced menus and distorted carols sung by squirrels on amphetamines, we contemplate with mixed feelings the hoards of people crowding the malls to buy "what Santa forgot."

Some see the shopping frenzy of the Christmas (and Chanukah and Kwanzaa) season as something to be frowned upon, a materialistic display incompatible with a religious holiday, but I see it as a sign of how blessed we are to live in a place that sells motion-sensing snow globes.

This is an incredible country. Hardly a day goes by that I am not reminded of the extreme wealth of this nation. I am not referring to wealth in the sense of gold chandeliers, diamond-encrusted shoes and butlers worth their weight in platinum. I am thinking about the stuff everyday Americans buy – and throw away.

Like computers. Our teenaged daughter is on her third laptop computer. (Thirteen years ago they hadn't even invented that dinosaur of operating systems, Windows 95.) We, as a country, can invent, build and buy sophisticated machines in such volume that we can afford to simply throw them away when they start giving us a little trouble. There is even a burgeoning industry devoted exclusively to chopping up obsolete computers and recycling the materials. I don't mean removing the hard drive and refurbishing the speakers. I mean smashing the computer to bits and sorting the different metals and plastics for re-melting and production of some new product.

Thanks to the institutions of private property and free enterprise, the 300 million American people have, collectively, a store of wealth the like of which has never been seen on Earth. "Store" is probably a bad choice of word because it implies a static pile of coins, like Scrooge McDuck's money vault. What the American people have is an economic engine that spews out a staggering array of goods and services in response to the demand of consumers.

You want not just a phone, but a cordless phone in pink plaid? You got it.

You want not just a doll, but a doll custom-made to look like your daughter? You got it.

You want not just a vacuum cleaner, but a vacuum cleaner with lights, filters, no cord and a programmable brain to make it sweep the floor by itself, on schedule? Fine, what color do you want?

And if it doesn't come in the color you want, fear not, the marvel of the free market system is that you can get it anyway. What about that one-of-a-kind, hand-knotted Oriental rug? You'd rather have it in blue? Can do.

No more Henry Ford, who would sell you a mass-produced automobile in any color you wanted, as long as you wanted black. Computers, to use our original example, come in every conceivable combination of features *and colors.*

Contrast America with the failed Communist model, where consumers queued up to buy "luxuries" – things we consider necessities. A Soviet model phone came in utilitarian black. And there was only one model available.

Americans would revolt at the idea that you couldn't buy a phone in chartreuse, mauve, scarlet or sand. Not only that, but the phone must have texting capability and Internet access, take pictures and movies, and include Bluetooth, a personal notebook and a movie library with 100 of your favorite films. It must also double as a laser pointer, a GPS guide and a spare TV remote. For $39.99, after rebates.

This is America, and, as at Alice's Restaurant, you can get anything you want.

But it's not having gee-gaws and gimricks in every color that makes me feel blessed at Christmas, it's what those gee-gaws represent. The country that has the intellectual energy to make robotic vacuum cleaners can make magnetic resonance imaging machines and cars with self-correcting skid systems. The country that has the financial resources to treat personal computers as disposable items can absorb the impact of terrorist attacks, catastrophic hurricanes and multi-billion-dollar wars.

So, every Christmas, even as I gag at the shelves full of shiny stuff and gawk at the bling, I feel thankful and blessed to live in a country where anything and everything is available. And while I do not wish to appear irreligious and materialistic, I really could use a pig-shaped talking rain gauge that dances and oinks when full.

I'd like that in apricot, please.

CHAPTER 14

College Admissions: Where Every Student Is Above-Average

There is going on, at this very moment, an elaborate mating dance involving your teenaged child. Every year, 18-year-olds and colleges engage in a ritualistic courtship culminating in an arranged union of the parties lasting approximately four years.

The students take classes and join clubs and play sports and do community service work to make themselves attractive to colleges, and the colleges woo students with letters, pictures, hats, posters and promises of financial aid.

The protocol of this courtship is so formalized it makes Kabuki theater look like improvisation. Gone are the days (the 1930s, to be exact) when, as my daddy says, "If you had $200, you could go anywhere you wanted."

Now students engage in a multi-year campaign to qualify for, apply to and be accepted by one or (preferably) more colleges. It is a grind from which they never recover, devolving into the famed "senior slump."

The typical college-bound junior will, in a high school with seven daily class periods, sign up for eight courses, three sports, two clubs and a part in the fall musical. Additionally, counselors insist that all students make Eagle Scout and perform 100 hours of community service a week.

Kids cling to the mantra, "I can sleep when I get old."

Having produced a suitably attractive portfolio in junior year, the student next searches for a college that is "a good fit." Counselors advise applying to a "reach" school, a bunch of schools the student has some interest in attending, and a couple of "safety" schools. Parents advise applying to a school that offers in-state tuition.

Students approach the process with varying levels of anxiety and interest. Some of them (the girls) fill out online profiles at college matchmaking websites, write dozens of essays months ahead of the deadline and apply to 12 or 15 schools. Others (the boys) find a school that doesn't require an essay as part of the application and …voila!

The colleges provide helpful information in the form of slick marketing brochures, virtual tours of the campus via CD and a succession of postcards touting their Rhodes scholars, championship football team and five-star dormitory accommodations equipped with Wi-Fi, laundry service, breakfast in bed, etc.

In the year that we had a child in the market for a college, we – or she, rather – received 28 pounds of unsolicited mail from colleges large and small, as well as inquiries from the armed forces. After awhile, she became quite blasé about colleges importuning her. One day she tossed something from Boston University in the trash. "I don't care what BU has to say. It's just a postcard. If it's not big and thick and says we think you're a genius, I'm not interested."

If colleges seem, from the brochures, all the same, students have a similar problem. They all have 4.0 GPAs, perfect SAT scores, letters in three sports, and a citation from the President for founding an organization that teaches homeless whales to read.

To help the admissions office sort things out, many colleges ask applicants to write an essay. The essay questions purport to probe the applicant's mind and mores, but only the boldest or blandest student would give a truly revealing answer.

Describe how you were moved, changed or unsettled by a work of art or literature.

"Seeing the Mona Lisa – or rather, not seeing it because it is encased in translucent bullet-proof glass and surrounded by a crowd of people so thick one thinks they are mannequins welded together – made me cynical."

Describe an incident in your life showing maturity or integrity.

"Usually I'm pretty immature, but Friday night when I used my fake

ID to buy a six-pack, I had the maturity to stop drinking when I got to the last can."

What is the meaning of life?

"Darned if I know."

No matter how dumb the questions, students agonize over answering them because they know the real question is:

Tell us something about yourself that will make the admissions officer reading your essay wake up with a snort, spew coffee all over your application and say, "Come on down!"

Somehow it all works out. The students and the colleges charge into a giant scrum together and emerge all paired off. The parents provide the dowry and the union is consummated.

As in any courtship, there is lots of angst. Collegiate anxiety peaks in January when applications are due and the admissions office learns if their marketing campaign was successful. Parental anxiety peaks at the same time, when parents are hounding their children to please please please complete the application and submit it. For students, anxiety peaks and breaks in April of their senior year, when colleges issue their invitations and students realize the hell of high school is over and they are IN COLLEGE! Time to party!

Whereupon, parental anxiety kicks in again.

CHAPTER 15

Super Bowl XL: Shocking Revelations

I often think how blessed we are as a nation to have an institution that so perfectly reflects the American psyche, our values, our attitudes towards family and friends, our patriotism, our deep attachment to tradition (by which I mean beer). I'm speaking of course about the Super Bowl.

When the Seattle Seahawks and the Pittsburgh Steelers take the field in Detroit on Sunday, a hush will fall over the land as the American people gather before the family shrine for the annual rite of winter.

Super Bowl Sunday has something for everyone, even people who (gasp) don't like football. For people who wear team jerseys and buy lava lamps in their team's colors, SBS is the holiest high day on the religious calendar. For people who think Seattle and Pittsburgh are merely large American cities, SBS is a day when they can pursue their favorite activity – golfing, bowling, hiking – certain that they will have the links/alley/trail to themselves.

Super Bowl Sunday easily eclipses New Year's Eve as a party event. There may be a million people in Times Square on December 31, but on February 5, 130 million people will be at Super Bowl parties, and they will focus on the show for a lot longer than it takes to watch a ball drop.

For that reason, SBS also eclipses Christmas. While other retailers experience a lull after Christmas, electronic stores enjoy a spike as fans stock up on giant screen TVs for the Super Bowl.

For many viewers, the ads are the best part. This is because oftentimes the game itself is boringly lopsided. This year, ads cost $2,500,000 per 30-second spot. Perhaps the only people who take the Super Bowl seriously are the execs who hope their multi-million-dollar message is clever enough to be the hot topic on Monday morning.

Scrooges and humorless left-wingers enjoy the Super Bowl extravaganza in a self-righteous sort of way. They sniff that all the money spent on the half-time production could be better used to rebuild the Gulf Coast or feed the starving Somalians, oblivious to the fact that in America, we can do both. We can indulge in a vulgar display of musical, marching, pyrotechnical exuberance costing millions of dollars, and it will represent only a fraction of the money we, as a people, have donated to disaster relief.

Nobody gets as worked up over football as America. For the rest of the world, it is soccer. Yeah, so the Brazilians, the Italians and maybe even the starving Somalians spend endless hours arguing over the World Cup. That doesn't compare to the Super Bowl. For one thing, the image of major soccer competitions is one of collapsing grandstands and patrons being trampled to death. Whereas the image of the Super Beer is…ooops, Freudian slip. The image of the Super Bowl is hot wings, pizza, Clydesdales in the snow, clashing gladiators, end zone celebrations, cheering crowds, insane young men covered in body paint and nymphets in costumes made out of discarded gum wrappers. What's not to like?

Although the charm of the Super Bowl for me is that every aspect of the event is over-the-top, there are people who miss the joke. For instance, Janet Jackson's famous wardrobe malfunction during the 2004 halftime caused a huge uproar. People who accept the barely-sanitized girlie show put on by the cheerleaders were shocked – shocked – to find that sexual titillation was an official part of the Super Bowl festivities.

These same people may also be surprised to learn that a lot of betting goes on, too. Super Bowl Sunday is one of the biggest betting days of the year. When I was on the Virginia Racing Commission, I once presided over a public hearing about whether to approve the construction of a racetrack in a certain county. One of the opponents said, "I have nothing against horse racing. I like horse racing. But why do you have to have gambling? Look how big pro football is and they don't have gambling."

There was a long second of stunned silence before the entire hearing room was convulsed with laughter. To their credit, even the speaker's fellow gambling opponents joined the laughter.

There is about the Super Bowl a giddy self-awareness, a delicious sense that this is an inside joke and we are all part of it. Outside of the players on the losing team, few people take the Super Bowl and the attendant hype seriously. Yes, billions of dollars change hands, hours of airtime and gallons of ink are devoted to it, and many of the related activities are in questionable taste, but, hey, this is The Super Bowl.

And nothing says "excess" like the Super Bowl.

This is the essence of Who We Are: People who apply all-American overkill to a nationwide party held on the flimsy pretext of watching a game.

Is this a great country or what?

CHAPTER 16

Tulips Are Nice, Four Lips Are Better

Valentine's Day has gotten out of hand. The image of St. Valentine's Day is cherubs, hearts and flowers, a frilly, serendipitous day of declarations of affection. In reality, Valentine's Day, like its evil twin, New Year's Eve, is a monster of unrealistic expectations and unfulfilled fantasies.

Valentine's Day has become a fiendish plot by Whitman's, Hershey's and whoever makes those tooth-chipping candy hearts. By advertising the holiday so heavily, they invest people with impossibly high hopes for True Love, thus setting them up for inevitable disappointment – disappointment that can only be assuaged by bingeing on chocolate.

The annual Day of Love has become hyped to the point that expressions of affection are no longer spontaneous but more of a command performance. Not only that, but there is a competitive angle to Valentine's Day gift-giving. The lacy card that once set hearts a-fluttering now engenders a mildly disappointed is-that-all-there-is feeling. Forget the construction paper and paper doilies. Nothing says "I love you" more than maxing out the plastic.

Single women feel they must have a serious beau on February 14, someone whose display of unrestrained passion can be flaunted in front of their friends. Married women feel they must receive a significant indication of spousal romance that can be worn like a badge in front of their friends.

(Note to guys: This is all about trophies.)

Men who are Valentine pros understand that women want the display of affection to be public. This is why the most romantic thing a guy can do is paint a girl's name on a water tower.

The whole event has become extremely stressful for women, which means that, by extension, it is stressful for men.

As the day approaches, women suffer increasing angst. Is he picking up my hints? Will he do something sufficiently brag-able? Has he noticed it's Valentine's Day?

The garment-rending anguish women experience seeps into the consciousness of their men, who find themselves thinking: What does she want? Can I afford it? What holiday is this? Are the stores closed yet?

Single women and brides spend the first 13 days of February fantasizing about the room full of roses, the wow-me bracelet and the erotic card with tickets to a Mediterranean cruise they expect to receive. Men spend the time making and collecting bets on the Super Bowl, wondering if there is enough tread left on the tires to get through the end of snow season and being briefly curious about repeated references to the neighbors' 1966 trip to Bermuda.

Smart women and women who have been married long enough do get over the competitive phase of Valentine's Day. This kind of woman understands that her man wants his True Love to be happy, but he's not a mind-reader.

True Love means giving men direct, simple instructions about your expectations, a day or two ahead of Valentine's. In fact, the nicest gift a woman can give a man at any time is a straightforward announcement of what she is thinking.

"I have spent the last six weeks sweating in the gym and subsisting on tofu and carrots so I will be more desirable for you. Please signify that you have noticed my new Barbie-doll figure by bringing me champagne and sexy underwear."

"Remember last year when I cried all day on February 15 because I thought your buying macadamia nuts meant you were secretly planning a trip to Hawaii? This year I'm thinking the burritos you had for lunch mean you're secretly planning a trip to Cancun. So plan a romantic getaway, even if it's only three hours at Motel 6."

"Sweetheart, you are always so dear about bringing me roses, but I have to confess that roses make me feel deeply inadequate. I can't make them open up and I get depressed as I watch their tightly-balled heads flop over and turn black. Even the artificial ones do that. But the tulips you brought me one time were fool-proof and made me feel fabulous – and deeply-loved. Roses, no. Tulips, yes."

Despite all the advertising about flowers, chocolate, jewelry and cruises, nothing beats a handwritten note expressing your affection. For the romantically-challenged among you, copy this in your own handwriting and leave it by the bed:

Roses are good, violets are fine, I wish that your lips were plastered to mine.

CHAPTER 17

Gold Medals for Serendipity

Snowboarding has taken the Olympics by snowstorm, possibly because the athletes themselves are so delightfully free-form, possibly because this is the winter sport more viewers can identify with. Many people snowboard and can appreciate what's involved. On the other hand, how many people do you know who go sledding 90 mph down an icy chute headfirst? Or who take their rifles cross-country skiing? An NBC online poll showed snowboarding as viewers' favorite sport (21.6 percent), with curling second (19.1 percent) and figure skating, the perennial leader, coming in third with 18.5 percent.

Curling's surprising popularity has nothing to do with the 2006 calendar featuring beautiful female curlers posing without their uniforms. (It's all very tasteful, of course, in keeping with ancient Scottish curling traditions. It's also sold out.)

Rather, curling got more air time this year and, for the first time, viewers could see for themselves the gut-wrenching, nail-biting, cliff-hanging appeal of the sport. Sort of like watching paint dry.

The Olympics always inspire a certain portion of the audience – mostly those consuming the Official Beer of the Olympics – to say, "I bet I can do that!" This is why visits to emergency rooms always spike during the Olympics.

One sponsor tapped into this phenomenon with a humorous commercial. In the ad, a middle-aged couple is inspired to try ice dancing on a pond one night, and the guy crashes into a shed, dislodging ice and snow from the roof which then fall onto his car, crushing it. I think that should be a new Olympic sport. Imagine the audience appeal: coed teams involving a girl in a skimpy costume AND cars getting wrecked. It would out-draw NASCAR and "Baywatch" combined.

It wouldn't be any more far-fetched than some of the sports they already have in the Olympics. The IOC requires that sports be played internationally before they are included in the Games. This is why, for instance, football and coon hunting are not Olympic sports.

However, it is really hard for me to believe curling is played widely enough to qualify. It looks like something they would dream up for "Saturday Night Live":

"Hey, let's mash a bowling ball and spin it around on an ice-covered shuffleboard and have a couple of players furiously sweep the ice in front of the ball while the spinner shouts instructions. And we have to come up with a totally random vocabulary, so that the announcer says things like, 'The skip's got some heavy ice on that rock. Would you look at that?! A biter! But they still have the hammer for the next end.'"

Et voilá! An Olympic sport is born.

Actually, I think that IS how it's done. Look at "boarding," as we cool insiders call it. One day, some boys are racing on their skateboards and one of them says, "Let's take the wheels off and see if it'll go on snow." And the next one says, "Yeah, and let's find a giant culvert and cut the top half off and tilt it and pack snow in it and do 720-degree flips." And the next one says, "Great! I'll go get my iPod!"

Because you can't do anything in the Olympics without your Personal Musical Device.

Apparently having your feet tied to a board, skimming over snow 30 miles an hour and turning flips 20 feet in the air isn't stimulating enough, so boarders plug into a little Fall-Out Boy to maintain their interest.

When Shaun White ("the Flying Red Tomato") won the half-pipe competition, the main thing all the wannabes wanted to know was, How many songs does he have on his iPod? (7,000)

Apparently Lindsey Jacobellis, the star female snowboarder, was listening to Fall-Out Boy during her medal-winning downhill race. As she approached the finish line, 100 yards ahead of her nearest competitor, she did a little celebratory hot-dogging...and fell. She got up and over the line in time to save second place. Her coach shrugged and said, "If you think what she did was wrong, you don't understand the sport."

Well, there are a lot of sports I don't understand.

But I do understand that Olympic sports have changed dramatically. The image of the Olympic athlete as an ascetic engaged in years of lonely, grueling workouts, training for that quadrennial opportunity to pit himself against the world's best for nothing but a laurel wreath is obsolete.

These kids are the gonzo graduates of the X-Games. They revel in inventing new, extreme sports. They are gregarious and colorful and push the envelope in all directions. They're fun to watch because they're having fun.

So go get your iPod. You've got the hammer for the next end.

CHAPTER 18

Puzzling over Priorities

My husband, Cricket, leaves the dresser drawers open. Not far, just a couple of inches. He leaves the closet door ajar, too. He deletes email without reading it. He doesn't eat the last, stale cookie in the bag before opening a new box of a better flavor. I, on the other hand, close dresser drawers, shut kitchen cabinets and fold up potato chip bags and put a clip on them. Not only do I open every email and read it, I respond, sometimes engaging in long discussions with people I don't know about things like the sheriff in Arizona who houses prisoners in tents. Cricket does not do any of that.

It used to bug me but lately I have come to admire Cricket for his ability to LET GO.

He likes to do crossword puzzles. The daily one he usually finishes with no problem, but the Sunday puzzle often has a few blocks that stump him. Then he gives it to me and I finish it.

I suppose we are well matched. I can't work a puzzle from the start, but I can fill in the last four or eight squares. He'll work it from the beginning, but – and this is the amazing and enviable thing about his personality – if he can't finish a puzzle, *he can put it down without a thought.*

Whereas I have this "tidy" gene that compels me to tie up all loose ends. I will spend all sorts of precious time completing meaningless projects, such as crossword puzzles. If Cricket hands me an unfinished puzzle, I feel an enormous responsibility to fill in those empty squares. They are an advertisement of the messiness of life, and, as a dedicated control freak, one who is determined to bring order into every corner of her world, I take it as my duty to fill in those squares! One Sunday Cricket left me about 16 squares, and I worked for an hour or so filling in three or four. After supper, I worked some more. Finally I went into my office and got out a stack of reference books – an almanac, a crossword dictionary, a Bible handbook, the New York Public Library Desk Reference, Bulfinch's Mythology, the encyclopedia (yes, we still have a hard copy), and an atlas. I stayed up past midnight and was worthless all the next day, but by golly, I finished that crossword puzzle.

Cricket is able not only to walk away from an unfinished crossword puzzle, he can throw away the newspaper without reading every word. Unlike some people we know, he doesn't let magazines he hasn't read and catalogues he's not going to order from pile up on the breakfront.

He lets go of things as well as tasks.

He can throw away a broken cereal bowl instead of putting the pieces in a closet for two years against the day when he might glue them back together.

When the day is done, he can stop working and relax. I can quit only when every square in the puzzle is filled, which happens…never.

Because I have such difficulty letting go, even when it comes to trivialities like crossword puzzles, I often get to the end of the day and feel frustrated that I have not done the things that are really important in my life. Usually that means not working on a writing project.

It's not that I don't have good role models for healthy behavior. In addition to Cricket, who is a paragon of priorities, there is my mother. She will finish the puzzle but isn't driven to get it right. As long as all the boxes have letters in them, she is satisfied. We all tease her about how she paints. She will paint a room one afternoon, slapping the brush this way and that without regard for the direction of the strokes. It may not bear close inspection, but it's done and she can watch "Law and Order" with a clear conscience.

Like Cricket, my mother is content because she knows what's important and she does that first and doesn't worry about the rest.

Even though I have had enough birthdays to identify closely with the adage about the futility of teaching a certain kind of dog new tricks, I do try to engage in a little self-improvement from time to time. Lately, thinking about all my birthdays, I have become aware that there is some limit to the number of candles my cake will accommodate, and so, hard as it may be, I have made up my mind to let go of trivialities and focus on the two or three really worthwhile things in life.

Even if a few squares of the puzzle remain empty.

CHAPTER 19

Supersnakewoman to the Rescue!

It's amazing how dangerous a little bit of knowledge can be.

One time my husband, Cricket, told me how to catch a snake and ever since then, I have felt like Robin the Reptile Wrangler.

The snake in the basement was a good-sized black snake who was coiled across the pipes in the rafters. "Go get a garbage can," Cricket told me over the phone from the safety of his office 25 miles away, "and knock him down into it with a broom handle."

The snake watched with interest as I attempted to position the can under him. As I picked up the broom and re-positioned the can several times, it occurred to me the snake might not cooperate. *I wonder what Plan B is,* I thought.

Miracles of miracles, all went as planned. The snake fell into the can, we transferred him to a 10-gallon aquarium with a screened lid, and Katie Bo took him to school for show-and-tell.

The height of my snake-handling career came when Katie Bo was about nine. Jonna Barber called in distress. A large black snake had appeared on the stone mantel of her new house. Would Robin the Reptile Wrangler come to the rescue?

I donned my supersnakewoman cape, grabbed a garbage can and the aquarium and was gone in a flash. Katie Bo went, too. Because of the can, we had to take Cricket's Chevy Blazer. This old vehicle, which I subsequently burned up on another memorable day, had a tailgate that was balky, and Cricket kept a screwdriver on the dash to operate latch.

Jonna's snake had slithered onto the bookshelves and wrapped himself around a stack of books. I set the garbage can on the counter just below the snake. Then, using a gaff hook, I pulled the snake, books and all, over the edge and into the can.

The avalanche of books knocked the snake silly, and I retrieved them (the books) easily. Although we had brought the aquarium, we had forgotten the water bowl, so I decided to leave the snake in the can until we got home. I opened the back of the Blazer with the screwdriver and pushed the can up behind the driver's seat.

Dum te dum dum. Gone from my mind was herpetologist Charlie Blem's stern warning, *Never...bring the snake into the boat with you.*

In my previous snake hunts, I had always, by chance, used smooth metal cans. But that night, I had grabbed a rubber can with molded ridges, the sort of shape and material that any self-respecting snake could get a purchase on.

We had driven a mile or so when Katie Bo sneaked a peek at the unconscious snake. "Mom!" she shrieked. "He's climbing up the side!"

Somewhat distracted by the need to steer the vehicle, I nevertheless reached behind the seat and hit the can as hard as I could.

A cautious peek by my sidekick revealed that the snake had been knocked back to the bottom of the can. But as she watched, the now-thoroughly-annoyed snake resumed his climb up the side of the can. More shrieks. More bangs on the can. More erratic driving.

After awhile, it dawned on me that I probably couldn't drive home with a snake trying to climb up the back of my neck, so I ordered Katie Bo to get the (unfortunately) rectangular lid of the aquarium, clap it over the can and shake the can violently, like people used to do when they were making popcorn. As she valiantly shook the can, I stopped the car and snatched the screwdriver to open the back. My poor panicked nine-year-old was shrieking "Mom! Hurry up!" and I was hollering, "Just keep shaking the can!" while I fumbled with the latch.

After an eternity, I got the back open and pulled the garbage can out. The snake, who was really furious now and had therefore developed adrenaline-powered climbing skills, was coming over the lip of the can and I was barely able to guide him into the aquarium in time. We clapped the lid on and taped it down with about three rolls of duct tape before either of us could relax.

It was a toss-up who was more frightened, Katie Bo or I. I maintain that I was in the most danger: Not only was the snake going to climb across my shoulder while I was driving, I had also opened myself up for a very damning "Mommy Dearest" book by Katie Bo one day. She has always been very gracious about the encounter, however, saying, "No, Mom, that wasn't nearly as bad as the time you wouldn't stop when the car caught on fire."

CHAPTER 20

Can You Say "Franchise" in English?

When we went to France one time a few years ago, I spent six months preparing to speak the language. I went to a tutor, listened to tapes and weeded the garden while practicing useful phrases such as, "Ma soeur a un crayon jaune…My sister has a yellow pencil." It turned out to be well worth the effort in that it produced several hilarious moments that my husband, Cricket, could later recount at cocktail parties.

While I have not needed to use my conversational French much since then, I have had other foreign-language collisions, usually at franchise food outlets. These establishments each have their own mysterious vocabulary of thematic names ("Rodeyodel Panwich") or pseudo-European terms ("Scoffle Churn") for burgers, fries and shakes. There is no handbook for the uninitiated customer – and no patience, either.

When we were in France, I always took a moment to compose my request in French before I entered a store or public transportation center. First I would think up the exact wording for what I wanted to say. Then I reviewed the applicable vocabulary words in case I had to engage in further dialogue with a clerk. Finally, I steeled myself, set my mouth and opened the door.

Sometimes it worked and we ended up with train tickets to the correct destination. And sometimes the nice French person would nod with a perplexed smile and say, "I think I would understand better if you spoke English."

My point exactly! I would understand a lot better if the fast food menu were in English.

After patronizing fast food places with a child for 10 years, I finally learned enough of the vocabulary to feel confident about ordering at one or two particular chains. So recently, when I went to Starbucks for the first time, I was pretty cocky about being able to order a cup of coffee.

Alas, Starbucks is even more daunting than burger houses.

I studied the overwhelming number of choices on the menu board and found one item, frappuccino, that I had heard our daughter, Katie, talk about. However, selecting the basic drink is only the first step. The thirsty patron must navigate several more decisions, because there are endless flavors, multiple sizes and various garnishes available. I started to get that panicky feeling inside. *What if I can't pull this off?* I thought. *You provincial rube.*

"Next?" said the clerk.

"Ma soeur a un crayon jaune."

"What?"

"I'll have a frappuccino," I whispered.

"That's cold, you know," she said.

It was a cold, rainy day and I wanted something hot, but I couldn't bear the thought of starting all over. "Fine," I croaked.

"What flavor?"

"Hmm. Vanilla."

"Whipped cream on top?"

"Oh, yes."

"Size?"

"Small."

Of course, Starbucks has bought into the rename-the-sizes thing. There is no "small." But "small" at Starbucks is not "medium" like it is at the burger place. No, "small" is called "tall."

My friend (you don't think I'd go to a new place alone, do you?) dazzled me with her *savoir faire* by ordering a "tall venti nonfat caramel macchiato."

Then I learned that you have to wait until they call out that your order is ready. Which means you have to know the shorthand for whatever you ordered. So we sat down to wait.

Pretty soon the clerk called out "venti skim carm mach" and my friend jumped up. And soon, after an elbow from my friend, I responded to "tall van cap."

I'm empowered now. I can go to Starbucks and order a "tall venti soy latte" -- or so I thought. This morning I went to Starbucks with Katie and managed (as I do quite regularly) to humiliate her with my ignorance.

As we waited in line, one of the clerks called for our orders. We approached the counter and said what we wanted. "Tall mocha latte" rolled smoothly off my tongue. So far so good. Then I held out a ten-dollar (!) bill, and the clerk said, politely, "If you'll take your place in line, you can pay at the register."

I looked around. "But I don't know where I was in line," I said pathetically.

Two people pointed to a spot on the floor. "Here."

So I went and stood there, feeling like George Costanza in line at the Soup Nazi's kitchen.

At least they let me buy the coffee.

CHAPTER 21

Staring at the Test Pattern

The last time I was at home, visiting my parents, they asked me to discipline the computer and make it do right. I slapped it around some, fixed the problem and, just for fun, changed the screen-saver. Previously, they had a sentence that scrolled across the screen, saying, "I love visiting Granma and Grampa!" I changed it to the one that shows pipes growing extensions and angles in different colors, building a rat's nest of plumbing all over the screen. Daddy, whose favorite pastime is to play Free Cell on the computer, remarked recently that he really liked the pipes.

"The engineers at GE all have that on their computers," my brother said.

Daddy nodded. "Yeah, sometimes I just sit and watch the pipes. Sort of like staring at the test pattern on TV."

Kids today don't know what the test pattern is, but it is something from the era of rotary dial phones and record players. It used to be there wasn't enough "content" to show on TV 24 hours a day, so about midnight or one o'clock in the morning, the TV stations would just sign off. (This worked because everybody in America in the 1950s went to bed by midnight.) They would play the national anthem with the flag waving against a blue sky and then go to the test pattern, accompanied by a buzz. In the black-and-white era, this was a bull's-eye design with the station's channel number in the middle. Later, a strip of colors ran down the side. Eventually some stations put up a sort of screen saver, usually the flag.

We used to joke about people being so dumb or drunk they would stare at the test pattern. Nowadays, people are so dumb they stare at the actual content, which, admittedly, is not as intellectually challenging as the test pattern.

The challenging part is working the remote control device.

Recently I read about some children who started a drive to collect old cell phones and have them reprogrammed for soldiers serving in Afghanistan and Iraq to use to call their families back home.

What I want to see is someone collecting old TV remotes and recycling them some kind of way. I'll bet if we all got together and threw our remotes into a big basket and then randomly fished out one for replacement, we would be just as well off.

What is it about TV remotes? The one that comes with the TV doesn't have some feature that you want – in my case that would be a mute button. So, you have to buy a generic remote – "TV toy" – to get the mute feature. But the new TV toy won't work the volume control, so you have to keep the original one handy for that. However, the original toy won't select the menu on a DVD, so if you want to rent a movie, you have to use the DVD player's toy to make it play. My parents have five TV toys laid out around the TV. We have four and I am resigned to watching whatever Cricket wants to watch because he and he alone can work the TV toys.

What's frustrating is to find that our daughter has had her laptop hooked up to the TV and changed the source code. I can't work the remote and the TV doesn't recognize my verbal commands to "Go back to the satellite!" so I start randomly, vainly pushing buttons on the side. Fooling with the TV and the satellite dish makes me understand how my parents feel about fooling with the computer.Recently, we had to get a technician to reprogram the TV upstairs. It is supposed to be on channel 73 to pick up the signal from the satellite receiver downstairs. However, this fancy new TV is so smart that when you plug it in, it programs itself for the local channels. It searches the sky and says, "OK, we get channels 6, 8, 12, 19, 23, 29, 35 and 57 here, so that's all I'm going to show." So when the homeowner (me) tries to put the TV on 73 so we can get the satellite, the TV smacks me on the wrist with his antenna and says, "No! No! We don't get 73 here!"

Sometimes it makes me want to go stare at the test pattern.

CHAPTER 22

How Many Ducks Could a Woodchuck Pluck?

Southerners are not always book smart, although a goodly number of them can read without moving their lips, but they are quite ingenious when it comes to solving problems. Some of this comes from living in rural areas where self-reliance is a part of the cultural heritage, and some of it comes from living in the path of hurricanes.

My friend, Buck Fevre, is a great example of Southern ingenuity.

One of the advantages of living in the country is that we each have our own well, powered by an electric pump, and we enjoy pure sweet natural water right from the tap. Of course, one of the disadvantages of living in the country is that when the power is out we have no water.

After Hurricane Isabelle wiped out all the trees and three-quarters of the power poles in Virginia, people in the country realized it would be next Tisha B'av before they had power again. You can cook on a gas grill and read by a lantern, but washing your clothes in the creek gets old fast, not to mention performing one's personal ablutions.

Buck and his boys are hardened woodsmen and hardly noticed the inconvenience, but Buck's wife is the flower of Southern womanhood, and he wanted to provide some civilized amenities (indoor plumbing) for her. It took some doing, but he solved the problem.

Buck has a gas pump that he uses to irrigate his garden and aerate the pond. He rigged it to pump water from the pond up to a barrel by the house. Then he ran a hose with a petcock from the barrel to the door. By the door was a five-gallon jug to fill and pour into the tank of the commode, as necessary. Sort of indoor-outdoor plumbing.

The truth is, Buck probably enjoyed the hurricane hardships because he delights in the challenge to improve his living conditions through the judicious application of technology.

Last year he decided to further his family's self-reliance by eliminating the need for cholesterol-reducing drugs, alarm clocks and trips to the grocery store, all in one fell swoop. Or coop. He built a chicken house and acquired some Barred Rock hens and a Leghorn rooster. So the cock crows in the morning (and a lot of other times, too, sort of like a digital watch beeping the hour), and the hens provide free-range, Omega-3, arterial-plaque-reducing eggs every day.

Buck has calculated that the chickens will pay for themselves in about 54 years.

Buck is, I understand, a pretty fair lawyer on the side, but in real life he is a hunter. One year, burdened with the chore of pulling pinfeathers out of a pile of waterfowl he and his boys had shot, he decided to mechanize the process. So he built a Rube Goldberg contraption called a duck-plucker.

He had in his possession a commercial duck-plucker, a rod with a sleeve of rubber fingers that, when twirled rapidly, beat the feathers off a duck. The rod can, apparently, be mounted on a drill bit. "But to do that you have to hold the duck in one hand and the drill in the other, so I thought I'd improve on it by mounting it on a table grinder," Buck said.

Note to readers: Do not try this at home.

One afternoon Buck gave me a demonstration of his inventiveness. Ushering me eagerly into his workshop, he showed me a plastic trashcan, sufficient in size to hold a lot of duck feathers. From one side of the can protruded a sort of funnel that might once have been a downspout. On the other side of the can, across from the funnel, Buck had attached his wife's old vacuum cleaner. This assemblage was placed in front of a table grinder, to which Buck had attached the rod with the rubber ducky-plucky thingies.

The whole thing looked like a medieval torture device.

To show me how it worked, Buck fetched a duck that he had handy. First he turned on the vacuum, then he turned on the grinder and held the duck up to it. The rubber thingies flapped around, beating the carcass and knocking the feathers off. A surprising number of the feathers floated near enough to the funnel to get sucked into the can, and the rest hung harmlessly around Buck's head and shoulders. "It's not the sort of thing you want to do in your living room," he hollered over the whooshing and grinding of the machinery.

I was really impressed with Buck's ingenuity, but I'm afraid I failed to convey that because I was laughing so hard. My guffaws were contributing to the dispersal of feathers all around the room, but I couldn't stop laughing long enough to apologize.

When I asked about the duck plucker recently, Buck shrugged and said, "It worked in theory."

CHAPTER 23

The Test of an Educated Citizen

I turned on the Internet recently and was stunned to read about a serial tragedy, right here in America, if you consider California part of America. The heart-wrenching story concerned some woman named Heather Locklear who was splitting up with her husband, Sambora, who is somehow connected to a guy named Bon Jovi. It turned out Heather was devastated to learn that Sambora was hooking up with her erstwhile best friend, Denise Richards, who lives next door and whose ex-husband-to-be, Charlie Sheen, is apparently hooking up with Sambora's previous ex-wife. I think I have this right.

Anyway, I gathered everybody involved was putting on a brave show in the face of all this pain, and they were all being civilized about it "for the children."

The whole thing was pretty shocking, and I read the article with a growing sense of alarm as I realized I had no idea who these people were. Here they were, Famous People on whom the future of Western Civilization depended – obviously, because they were presented with screaming headlines and grainy photos shot through a telephoto lens by a photographer trying to avoid being stomped by the Famous Person's bodyguards – and I was clueless.

Shortly after this disturbing event, I received further evidence of my cultural ignorance. In a conversation with a teenager, I was challenged to name three rap people. I confidently reeled off, "Eminem, M C Hammer and Toby Keith." She laughed derisively, claiming that Hammer was a hip hop person, but I insisted Hammer counted because there are really only three kinds of music: Frank Sinatra, Country & Western, and Other. Hip hop, rap, ska, karaoke – they're all indistinguishable to me, so I claimed half a point for Hammer. (She rejected TK completely despite the fact that he did a piece called "(I Wanna) Talk about Me" that definitely was a rap-inspired experiment, one that he wisely decided not to repeat.)

So once again I had failed the test of an educated citizen.

I've always admired the example of essayist Calvin Trilling and his wife, Alice. They felt an obligation, as educated citizens, to keep up with important issues both home and abroad. However, they soon realized there was more news in the world than either of them could absorb, so they divided things up. I imagine today, for instance, he is reading the news reports on the suffering in Darfur, illegal immigration in America and Iran's nuclear ambitions. She, meanwhile, is following the unrest among unassimilated immigrants to France, the impact of the growing Indian and Chinese economies on the global oil supply and any natural disasters worldwide, especially in the Gulf of Mexico.

In that vein, I keep up with professional tennis, horse racing and the NFL and let my husband, Cricket, keep up with Ted Kennedy, Condi Rice and the NY Yankees. Meanwhile, Katie does movies, TV and music videos and gives us a distilled version when we need to fill in a crossword puzzle. This system has worked well for many years, and I have felt confident, thanks to the presence of a teenager in the house, that I was pretty much up on pop culture. Sadly, I have been over-confident.

So I made a bold decision to catch up on my own.

After immersing myself in the media that catalogue the affairs of people made famous by their performances on TV, in the movies, in concert or in court, I have learned many fascinating factoids, none of which remains with me long enough to repeat.

The truth is, even with such valuable tools as "People" magazine, cable TV and the Internet, it is hard to keep abreast of the important issues of the day. Every story seems to involve Female Celebrity #1, Female Celebrity #2, Male Celebrity #1, Celebrity of Indeterminate Sex #1, and several spokespersons and attorneys. After their 15 minutes of fame, I can't keep them straight. So I've given up.

I once wrote a column about how my friends laughed at me because I didn't know which celebrity went on the Famous Fat Person's Magic Diet and which one had her stomach stapled. "Oh!" my friends said, "You don't have cable!"

Well, now we have a satellite dish and I still don't know who Heather Locklear is. But, thanks to the dish, and a news show called "West Wing," I do know that Charlie Sheen's father has MS and he used to be the President. Not only that, Alan Alda's a Republican!

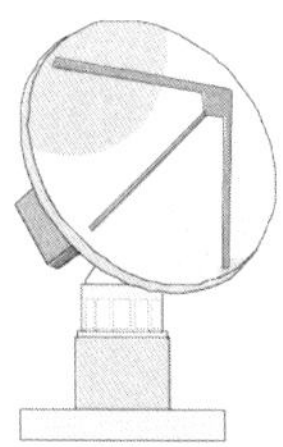

CHAPTER 24

Numbers You Can Relate To

The TV news reported in 2008 that some governmental authority had calculated the federal deficit for the year to be 465 billion dollars. "However," the newscaster continued in a tone of voice suggesting that he expected all of us to take this seriously, "the Congressional Budget Office says the deficit will be only 455 billion dollars."

So, they were off by a trillion dollars. Close enough for government work.

My brother Bo and I were discussing this revelation and he said, "Gosh. If I had a trillion dollars, I'd get new tires for my truck and, well, I don't know what all."

My husband, Cricket, hollered in from the other room that we had it all wrong, the difference between the two deficit estimates was one percent of a trillion. So Bo said, "What's one percent of a trillion? Well, then, at least I could get the front end aligned."

Okay, clearly, I don't know what a trillion is. And frankly, I don't know what a billion is, either, but I did some research.

Thanks to the Internet, I have an email here that says – (and you know you can trust any information you get over "the Internet" because it's spelled with a capital "I") – "A billion seconds ago, it was 1959. A billion minutes ago, Jesus was alive. A billion hours ago, our ancestors were living in the Stone Age. A billion dollars ago was only eight hours and 20 minutes, at the rate Washington spends it."

Clearly, that was written before the Obama Administration took over and substituted "trillions" for "billions."

There used to be a U. S. Senator names Everett Dirksen who was famous for saying, "A billion here, a billion there, and soon you're talking about real money."

Real money to me would be paying for a candy bar with folding money. One time when our daughter, Katie Bo, was about five, she wanted some novelty candy item in a convenience store. "A dollar ninety-eight," the clerk said, and I about fell out. Katie Bo turned to the clerk and said confidentially, "My mother thinks everything ought to cost 25 cents."

When I learned that the OMB and the CBO were more than a trillion-with-a-T dollars apart in their deficit estimates, I immediately thought about Senator Dirksen. And when Cricket corrected my math and I learned that the OMB and the CBO were only *one percent* of a trillion-with-a-T dollars apart in their deficit estimates, it just confirmed my thinking that any number over about a hundred is pretty nearly incomprehensible to us mere mortals.

Remember when you were small and counting to a hundred was a major milestone? Nowadays, school children have calculators because they don't have time to count up to a billion. But just because you can define a billion doesn't mean you understand how much it is. You have to break big numbers down into smaller numbers you can relate to. Something you can count to. Like 100.

It's easy to comprehend single digits. One odd penny. Two world wars. Three cars. Four seasons. Five gold rings. A six-pack of beer. Seven cats (yikes!). Eight Crayola crayons. Nine baseball players.

Double digits are comprehensible, too. I can, for instance, understand that I have had 56 birthdays, especially the morning after I've played a two-hour tennis match.

10 fingers. 11 football players. 12 eggs. 13 days without power after Hurricane Isabel. 87 trees per block down after Hurricane Isabel.

Triple digits are still manageable. 100 pennies. 365 days. 135 miles to The Beach.

Four digits are starting to stretch my brain. Taking 2,112 steps to jog a mile.

Five digits would cover my salary at my last job. But I really couldn't relate to that entire number, so I always thought of the amount of take-home pay in each paycheck. The same goes for six-digit numbers. The average mortgage is thought of in terms of the monthly payment. The car with 200,000 miles got there at three, four, five hundred miles a week.

Do you see the pattern here? As soon as you get over three digits, you want to break the number down into smaller bites so you can relate to it. Smaller, marshmallow-y bites.

And really, relatively small numbers contain more wow factor than the ones with buckets of zeros. Speaking of marshmallows, one night our daughter had a party, and two boys (note sex) had one of those competitions only guys would have. The winner, who shall be nameless here, stuffed 13 marshmallows into his mouth before spewing them out in the yard.

Now that's a number I can relate to.

CHAPTER 25

A Salute to Independence Day

We spent Independence Day quietly. A little yard work, a little tennis from Wimbledon, a steak on the grill. I beat the birds out for some wild blackberries, and we had a delicious, experimental cobbler that I'll never be able to replicate. Mother Nature provided the fireworks – vivid flares complete with the kettle drums and cymbal clashes of the 1812 Overture.

We don't save our patriotism for a single day in summer, we wear our national pride every day, so the Fourth of July is more a reflective day for us than a whoopin' and hollerin' holiday. This year in particular we passed the day not with a big celebration of an historical event but in quiet appreciation of the transition from dependence to independence.

Independence Day began with a 4 a.m. phone call announcing that our sort-of-independent child had arrived in Another Country. Since, from our point of view, she was safe and, from her point of view, safely beyond our reach, we all slept well and awoke to a bright new day.

Our 18-year-old has always been one to think for herself, but her departure for a month abroad, to be followed almost immediately by her departure for college, marks a new stage in her evolving independence. "Exploding" independence might be a more appropriate word.

Like the brash New World colonies, Katie is a young energetic restless representative of a new generation. Like the colonies, yearning to be free from out-dated laws dispensed in heavy-handed fashion by an authority figure far removed from the reality of the scene, Katie has chafed and struggled against parental limits. She hasn't had a party and dumped our Maxwell House into the James River, but we've had a few skirmishes.

Unlike King George, we recognize – and welcome – the inevitable.

We're all trying to resolve this through diplomacy instead of using the nuclear option. She respectfully announces her intentions, pointing out her resume of Good Choices. We solemnly announce we are giving her a little more rein, maintaining the fiction that we could, somehow, hold her back by force. It is only mutual love that holds the gossamer reins to the bit.

One day when she was about nine, Katie was whining about all the work she had to make up after missing a whole week of school. "Why can't you just start work when you're in the fourth grade? I mean, you already know 'most everything. You can read and comprehend and you can do enough math to figure things out. Why can't fourth grade just be college and you can go to work?"

Amazingly, to us, it seems as though she has leaped from fourth grade to college. She's already been to work, so she's reached a certain stage of independence. Now, as she leaves home, we are all experiencing new freedoms.

For us, Fourth of July was a day of freedom from worry waiting for the child to come home because she isn't here. For her, it was freedom from calling home and arguing about how late she could stay out and where she could go.

Independence means:

Freedom to drive too fast and pay for your own speeding tickets.

Freedom to find out how many tequila shooters you can balance on top of rum punch and shrimp scampi.

Freedom to burn the candle at both ends and learn for yourself that one can of Red Bull, while it may get you through the morning, is not the equivalent of a lost night of sleep.

In other words, the freedom to make your own mistakes. (Parents' plea: Just try not to make any irreparable ones that you will regret later, like getting tattooed, pregnant or convicted of a felony.)

Of course, her departure means we will have to become independent ourselves:

Backing up the computer by burning data on a CD.

Remembering to leave an "away message."

Learning how to order at Starbucks.

Keeping up with pop culture so we can finish crossword puzzles.

Independence isn't all about making mistakes. It's about opportunities, too. Now Katie has the opportunity to explore the world, meet strange new people, think un-thought-of ideas and live a rich, full life.

And Cricket and I have the opportunity to pick up where we left off 18 years ago, enjoy each other, travel, buy a boat and, maybe, get some sleep.

CHAPTER 26

Husbands to the Rescue

Although I would like to think our family is like the Cleavers in "Leave It to Beaver," the truth is, the TV sitcom we most closely resemble is "I Love Lucy." If Lucille Ball were reincarnated and wanted to write some new episodes, Buck Fevre's wife, Dotty, and I have decided she could use us for inspiration.

The plot was always the same: Lucy would take it into her head to do something – redecorate the entire house or learn to be a tap dancer – that she knew her husband, Ricky, would disapprove of, so she would figure a way to get it done behind his back. She always envisioned presenting him with the *fait accompli* and proudly telling him, as he gazed in amazement at the results of her cleverness and efficiency, that she had saved a bundle. Of course, it never turned out that way. Lucy would get tangled up in endless rolls of wet wallpaper, knock over the ladder with the paint bucket and be crying on the floor when Ricky came home.

"Lucy," Ricky would begin in that ominous Cuban accent, "you got some 'splainin' to do."

"Oh, Ricky," she would wail, "I was just trying to make you happy and save some money."

In the end, Lucy's loving husband would melt and rescue his darling bride. The house got redecorated, but it cost Ricky a bundle.

Like Lucy, Dotty and I are always starting projects that we know our husbands won't approve of, then we hit a snag and have to ask for their help. In my case, Cricket is frequently having to rescue me from farm chores gone awry.

One time I was determined to fertilize the pasture, but I didn't know how to hitch the equipment to the tractor. Then I learned that the feed store rented out a fertilizer wagon that didn't need the tractor's PTO. They would fill it with customized fertilizer and you could pull it around the pasture with a pickup. Cricket had already told me in no uncertain terms fertilizing would have to wait until he took care of 47 other chores around the place. I was thrilled that I could get the fertilizing done without bothering him, and, like Lucy, I envisioned presenting him with fertilized fields and receiving his grateful praise.

Of course, it didn't turn out that way. The day I knew Cricket would be gone long enough for me to get the job done came after a heavy rainfall. I stubbornly pressed ahead, hauling the wagon 15 or 20 yards before getting bogged down in the mud. The wagon was fully loaded and the non-four-wheel-drive truck could not pull it out of the morass.

I wasn't sitting on the floor crying when Cricket came home, but I felt like it. We had to wait a couple days for things to dry out, paying extra rent on the wagon, of course, and then it took Cricket two more days to get the tractor running, unhitch the truck and pull it out, hitch up the wagon and pull it out, then spread the fertilizer with the tractor.

The pasture got fertilized but I definitely had some 'splainin' to do.

Dotty Fevre's mishaps usually involve moving furniture, and I have often played the role of Ethel, helping rearrange Lucy's furniture to disguise the new sofa she wasn't supposed to buy.

Once Dotty acquired an enormous dresser that seemed perfect for a bedroom upstairs. Buck had reasonably pointed out that the 10-ton dresser could not be carried up the narrow, turned stairs, even by the Olympic gold medal weight-lifting team. But Dotty believes, correctly, that Buck can do anything she needs him to do. Thus inspired, he and the boys managed to get the dresser upstairs and into the bedroom without knocking down the railing or scraping off too much paint.

The only problem was, once she saw the dresser in the bedroom, Dotty knew it was wrong wrong wrong. She had the wit not to say so while Buck and the boys were still panting from the exertion, but it preyed on her mind. So one day when Buck was out of town, she browbeat the boys into helping her bring the dresser back downstairs. But when they tried to lift it over the newel post where the stairway turns, the dresser got stuck in the narrow stairwell, and they couldn't get it up or down. For a couple of days, until Buck got home, the boys had to crawl under the dresser to get to their rooms.

When you're having a Lucy moment, the worst part is anticipating your husband's discovery of your predicament.

I'm told that Buck does an excellent Cuban accent.

CHAPTER 27

Keeping Chickens

I look on keeping chickens sort of like I look on cigarette smoking: It's such a nasty habit, but it's still legal, so I guess we have to let people do it.

My mother has always loved chickens. We had chickens when I was growing up and they were always hanging around in the yard, making a mess on the walk, and fluttering through the stall door spooking the horses. My brother thought they were so tacky he wouldn't let any of his friends come visit. And I vowed never to have fowl of any kind when I grew up.

Of course, now I realize that the shortcomings of keeping chickens can be minimized by building a coop and penning them up some of the time.

We have several friends who are keeping chickens under those circumstances and it seems to be working out all right. Susie Salsitz, who has a fabulous house full of cool things she has designed, painted or somehow crafted, has an equally fabulous chicken house. She keeps exotic chickens with long curly feathers – the kind my daddy calls "frizzly chickens" – so she had to build an elegant chicken coop in keeping with their image.

My friend Buck Fevre keeps chickens, too. He has conventional laying hens in a conventional coop. His wife, Dotty, has revealed to me, however, that he lets them out on work-release from time to time, which I guess makes them semi-free-range chickens. But she, too, has the problem of keeping the messy birds away from areas where the free-range humans roam.

Keeping chickens, like smoking, is a compulsive behavior that spreads to other parts of your life. Neither chickens nor smokers can be contained for long. When you have chickens, before long you find you have progressed from "keeping chickens" to "being in the poultry business."

In Buck's case, it all started with a broody hen. Among his flock of hens was one of such determination that she was obviously descended from the original wheat-growing, bread-baking Little Red Hen. This hen did not want to donate her eggs to the breakfast plates of Buck's boys. She wanted to hatch them, so she sat on the nest and objected to being removed with an impressive display of fluttering, squawking and pecking. Buck didn't want her to have a brood of chicks, he just wanted her to lay eggs, so he made all sorts of barriers to prevent her from setting on her eggs. But she would climb over whatever barrier he had contrived, and against all odds, she would get back to set on her eggs, dammit. Finally, he surrendered to the imperative of Nature and built her a separate home for unwed mothers.

The home for broody hens consists mainly of an A-frame made of chicken wire. "It's called a 'chicken tractor,' for reasons I don't fully understand as it looks like a tent with wire over it," said the intrepid poultryman, who added that he had modified the classic design to include a surplus dogloo for shade. "I'm sort of making this up as I go along."

Buck gathered a clutch of eggs and put the little red hen in the dogloo with a nest. "She sat on six eggs and hatched five. They were all different because we have different hens. She had four Barred Rocks and one little red hen. The little red hen is my favorite."

After a suitable period of maternity leave, the hen was removed to the main coop. As for the chicks, he says, "They're still growing. Eventually, they could be the beginning of your flock," he offered.

Not unless my husband goes back to smoking.

Buck may be giving his chickens away now, but the next thing you know, he'll be in the business, selling them nationwide as my mother did. Many years ago Momma had some game chickens, which she decided to sell commercially as a supplement to the family budget. She ran an ad in "Grit and Steel," the national journal of game fowl, offering a trio for $12, and it wasn't long before the phone in Virginia started ringing. However, the customers were all from Oregon (like, they don't have chickens in Oregon?).

Every time Momma made a sale, Daddy recalls, he took off half a day from work, bought $30 worth of lumber and built a shipping crate for the rooster and two hens. Then, because Mailboxes Etc. and Federal Express had not been invented, Daddy drove the crate of chickens to the train station and paid to ship them across the country.

"The long and the short of it was, your momma would get the $12 and I would be out about $50," he said.

He couldn't say much about her bad habit, though, because he smoked like a chimney.

CHAPTER 28

Save the Endangered Trash!

I have here on my desk an old digital camera – "old" being a relative term, you understand. I have a loaf of bread older than this camera. Once upon a time, this camera could look out on the world and sense the light and shadows. It could memorize a picture and convey it to a computer in a grid of tiny dots – "pixils." But no more. When you push the power button, the camera purrs agreeably, the zoom lens pops out and an astonishing array of hieroglyphics appears on the screen. Then, without any prompting whatsoever, the camera pulls its zoom snout back in, douses the hieroglyphics and shuts off. No amount of button-pushing, batteries or begging will induce the camera to perform any other maneuvers.

It is utterly useless. It won't take pictures – which even the most primitive cell phone will do today – and it would cost more to fix than to replace.

Actually, I have already replaced it with a model that I like better, but the defective one sits on my desk. Once in awhile, I pick it up and turn it on, watching foolishly as the zoom pops out and in and the camera shuts down. Einstein said the definition of insanity was doing the same thing over again, expecting a different result.

Yet, I cannot throw it away.

I am still too close to the day when such a device was a technological marvel, a fine piece of engineering and miniaturization available as a luxurious by-product of the space program. How can something so complex be disposable?

In a word or three, the Great American Economy. See what the free enterprise system hath wrought.

Our daughter takes it for granted because it is all she has ever known. While I have never known want, I was raised frugally by children of the Depression. Their constant admonitions to conserve – use it up, wear it out, make it do or do without – burned into me the notion *Don't waste!* Depression era folks won't get rid of anything, including a body part, until it is completely worn out. When my mother's 80-year-old hip joint gave out, she agreed to replace it with a nice new titanium one. But she wrung every bit of use out of the old one first, dancing in pain on New Year's Eve the week before her surgery.

What with growing up with Depression-era parents and coming of age in the Sixties (Earth Day, etc.), I have learned the lessons of conservation and recycling too well. Not only am I reluctant to chuck malfunctioning electronic devices, I subconsciously look at every item with a view to reuse. Far be it from me to waste anything that might have the slightest value to some unknown person on the far side of the globe.

I *believed* the connection between cleaning my plate and saving starving children in China.

So I save everything. I once read a mental health column about people whose houses are so full of stuff they've "saved" that the rescue squad can't find them when they have an emergency. That's going to be me. There's even a name for it: Compulsive Hoarding Disorder. The article listed the most common things that people with CHD save, and I save all of them!

The article listed: old newspapers or magazines (I collect both), old mail (check the floorboard of my car), catalogs (items I will never order are marked), old appliances (out in the garage), broken knickknacks (gonna fix 'em some day), fast-food restaurant condiment packets (why buy a bottle of catsup?), sewing fabric (several closets), wishbones from chickens (and turkeys), and shoes (Imelda Marcos, eat your heart out). The article also listed "cats" as something people hoard, but we have only four, so maybe I'm safe there.

I have a drawer full of all the sales tickets from all the clothes I've ever bought at Talbots. In another drawer, I have all the shoulder pads I've taken out of all the clothes I've ever bought at Talbots. I have also saved the clothes I wore on significant occasions: my last wedding, the 1974 Submarine Birthday Ball at Pearl Harbor, the day Judge Wilkerson decided not to send me to jail, etc.

There is no solution. Compulsive Hoarding Disorder is a heartbreaking, incurable affliction. So I keep the old digital camera on my desk and console myself that I'm not alone. Next time you pass a mini-storage place, think about all the people who pay monthly fees to store broken digital cameras and stacks of old newspapers that their Depression–era parents wouldn't let them throw away.

On the bright side, think of all the landfill space we're saving.

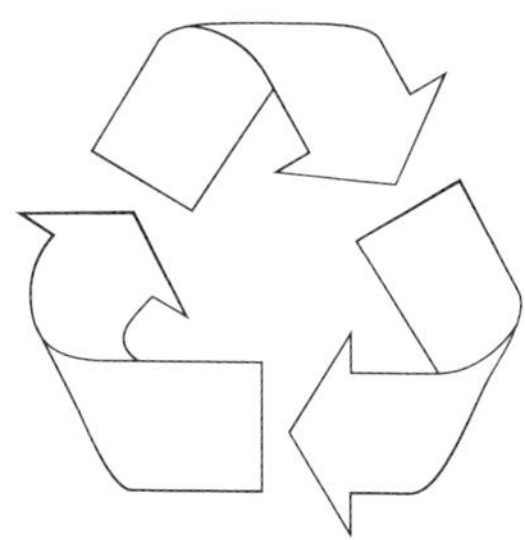

CHAPTER 29

Daddy's Little Princess

It's sort of hard to imagine now, but our tomboy in riding boots and a ball cap once aspired to be crowned a beauty queen. Katie was about 11 when she showed us an ad for a local pageant and said, "Can I do that?"

Not my thing, I thought, but what can it hurt?

So I called the organizer to ask a few questions. She was very reassuring. I gathered this was a sort of "starter" pageant for girls (and their clueless moms) to learn the ropes. The costs, she assured me, were minimal. Katie could wear her regular clothes. "This is not a glitz-and-glamour pageant," she told me several times. I gathered that was a good thing.

At some point, she suggested maybe we should get a coach.

Whoa, I thought. But then, I had grown up on the horse show circuit. Remembering how we used to laugh at the guy riding a Western saddle in an English class, I said, "Okay, give me the coach's number."

So then we made an appointment with the coach for Katie to learn to walk. The coach would also evaluate her wardrobe.

The coach's daughter had been on the circuit for 15 or 20 years, and their house was full of curio cabinets with crowns, tiaras, sashes, trophies and portraits. In one place, there was a sort of shrine, with trophies, pictures and laminated news articles from various pageants arranged on stepped risers.

We had clearly come to the right place.

The coach gave Katie a quick stage lesson. She told her where to stop and turn, where to stand and smile, how to place her feet. I drew the pattern on the back of an envelope. I didn't care whether Katie won or not, but I didn't want people laughing at her for using a Western saddle.

"Do you have a gown?" she asked and I showed her the Sunday school dress I (hilariously) imagined Katie could wear in the gown competition.

I'm sure the coach was wondering, privately, how this poor child would stand a chance with such an ignorant mother, but she patiently showed us what the judges would be looking for: a miniature replica of the frothy white gown Lady Diana wore when she married Prince Charles.

This, it turns out, was what Katie was looking for, too. She tried it on and was immediately captivated.

As Katie admired herself in the mirror, I picked up an orange satin jumpsuit covered with sequins and said, "So sometimes the girls wear pantsuits in the gown portion?"

No, the coach said, trying to use one-syllable words, that's for sportswear.

After the coaching session, I returned all the clothes we'd bought and started over. We struck a deal with the owner of the wedding cake dress and rented it for the show. We also bought a lot of hair products, and I experimented with curling Katie's long hair. I mailed Katie's entry form, entering her in all the optional portions, too – photogenic, talent, etc. So much for "minimal" costs.

The pageant was held at the high school, where, fortuitously, Katie made friends with a little girl who was a veteran. The little girl cheerfully shared bobby pins, hairspray and advice throughout the day. Katie had a wonderful time. She walked the walk and turned the turns.

Meanwhile, my husband and I sat in the audience, mesmerized. As we were watching chubby little tots twirling batons and tap dancing, Katie suddenly materialized next to us. "Daddy!" she said in a voice cracking with anxiety. "You've got to go home *quick* and get the piano!"

Our coach had told us that showing a video of Katie riding her pony probably wouldn't work for the talent portion. So Katie, who had been force-fed piano lessons for a few months, had planned to play something from her repertoire. We assumed the high school had a piano.

As Katie trembled in fear that her magical day would end in humiliation, her dad smiled and pointed to a piano tucked in a corner, obscured by a pile of coats. Katie exhaled.

Several girls sang and danced to Broadway show tunes. Katie plonked out her forgettable tune. Eventually, the interminable day drew to a close. Katie looked lovely in the rented wedding dress, the two cans of hairspray maintained some of the curl in her hair and she received a truly impressive trophy for being third runner-up.

But the moment that brought a tear to my eye was when Katie expected her father to run home and toss the piano in the pickup so she could perform. I loved the fact that she *knew* he could do such a thing, in the next 15 minutes.

This was the biggest moment of her life and there was a huge problem, but she knew who could fix it.

Dad.

CHAPTER 30

Parking Lot Vultures

You see them cruising slowly up and down the aisles of the parking lot, circling the lines of parked vehicles like kids playing musical chairs: inching slowly past the cars with people unlocking doors, speeding up around the corners to follow a person laden with bags. But this is no child's game. They have a predatory look in their eyes as they scan the rows, visually feeling each trunk for the telltale vibration of a car in reverse. Their right foot pats the pedal, ready to outgun any competitor and pounce on the prize.

They are Parking Lot Vultures, ruthlessly hunting the Perfect Parking Place.

And what, pray tell, constitutes the Perfect Parking Place? The PPP is, first and foremost, close to the entrance. It must be the closest spot available within the cruising time limit. The cruising time limit is a personal variable and constitutes the Great Unknown when one vulture is competing with another.

Searching for the PPP can become a tension-filled undertaking that easily eclipses the purpose of the trip. Do you take the first open space, which may be as far as eight or nine slots out from the coveted but *verboten* handicapped spaces? Or do you drive around for 15 minutes in hope of finding a slot two or three spaces closer? -- 15 minutes during which you could have gone in the store, selected a shirt, tried it on, called your best friend for advice, decided to buy it, paid for it and left? Trade-offs are inevitable. How much is your time worth? Are you fit enough to walk the 24 extra feet three more slots would demand?

Only the strongest, most competitive vultures survive the strain of battle. Notably, some of the fiercest Parking Vultures are found competing for parking places in front of the fitness center.

Like bank robbers, some Parking Vultures feel that ease of departure trumps access to the entrance. Thus, the pull-through: the exquisite point at which two parking spaces end-to-end are available, allowing the driver to pull through the first one and be positioned to drive away from the second one without engaging reverse gear.

Others find that having two spaces side by side is the most attractive option. These are the people driving oversized vehicles with the turn radius of the space shuttle, people who find it hard to figure out where to make the turn to end up between the striped lines.

Parking Vultures are older than shopping malls. All Parking Vultures today are descended from the original group of drivers who couldn't parallel park downtown and had to drive around the block until they found a space on the end.

My dad has mellowed a bit in recent years, but he was the Alpha Male of the Parking Vultures for decades. He drove a big car, and he would dare anybody to match fenders with him for a good parking place. He was obsessed with finding the PPP, sometimes trying one and then backing out in favor of another one – closer to the door, shaded in the afternoon, out of the way of falling meteors, whatever.

We spent many years on the horse show circuit, and whenever we arrived at a show, Daddy would scour the grounds for the best place to park, often trying out two or three places. He'd find a nice shady spot, let the engine idle and say, "You know, we're liable to get boxed in by the other trailers here." So he'd pull our rig around to another place. "No," he'd say, "we'll be in the sun in the afternoon." More trundling around the showgrounds. Just as I'd start to open the door, he'd say, "This is bad. Now we've got to go all the way over yonder to get water." The horse and I would both be carsick by the time he settled on a place.

It's probably no surprise that my parents met when Daddy was trying to beat Momma out for the perfect parking place.

They were both headed for the Officers' Club at Ft. Benning, Georgia, that fateful day.

"The first parking space belonged to the general, but I saw the next one to it was open," said Daddy. But, there was another car, poking along, threatening perhaps to take *his* parking space.

"I didn't know where I was," Momma said, "and this upstart behind me was honking the horn."

"So I squeezed around real quick and took that parking space," Daddy recalled.

He was outraged that she would aim for his spot, but he reconsidered when he saw how cute she was.

CHAPTER 31

Programming the Mental Computer

I knew I was spending too much time on the computer when I wrote a thank-you note in longhand and paused to see if a red line would appear under a word I thought I had misspelled.

We laugh about programming people to do things, but the mind is an amazing, self-programming computer.

It doesn't take but one time of stubbing your toe to program your mental computer with a grid of where the legs of the sofa are.

The most graphic evidence of that I've had recently came from the optician at Wal-Mart who filled my prescription for progressive lens. Progressives are sort of like bifocals, only worse, since the optical correction changes progressively from top to bottom. The optician told me they would be hard to get used to, but he urged me to put them on and wear them all day. "It takes a week or two for the computer in your brain to be programmed, but after that, you won't notice a thing."

Actually, it took only a few days for my mind to make all the adjustments. I could turn my head to look at something without have to shift up and down to find the right area to look through. I was amazed.

But of course there are bugs and glitches in the software occasionally. For instance, when I've been driving my stick-shift car for awhile and I get in a car with automatic transmission, I find myself jamming on the brake with my left foot, looking for the clutch.

Then, too, if your mind is still operating on one of those early languages – Fortran, Cobal, Pig Latin – sometimes you don't have enough memory for the upgrade.

Like a lot of Baby Boomers, I fantasize about recapturing my youth and playing my favorite sport at a professional level against 20-year-old guys who are awed when I bring my good stuff and who beg for my training secrets. As part of that self-delusive effort, I take tennis lessons from a young guy named Patryk who does an impressive job of pretending we are working towards my debut at Wimbledon. He does this by telling me, with a straight face, things to do, such as, "react to the ball sooner." Sweetheart, I want to tell him, if I could program my brain (not to mention my body) to do that, I really could go on the pro circuit.

I can't even reprogram my brain to lace up the new tennis shoes I bought to wear at Wimbledon. In the old days, people laced tennis shoes (pronounced *tinnie* shoes) up through the bottom of the holes. To tighten them, you grabbed the laces on top of each pair of eyelets and pulled. But now shoes come with a different pattern of lacing. The new pattern is, really, easier to tighten, because all you have to do is pull with one finger in the middle at each place where the laces cross. But I cannot teach my fingers to do that. They still try to pull the laces at the eyelets and then the laces get all tangled and I despair of ever making it to Wimbledon.

My dad used to travel a lot in his business, sometimes driving as much as 50,000 miles in a year. By February every year, his mental computer was programmed to operate the car on autopilot, and he drove at least 10,000 miles a year while snoozing. Daddy would come home and laugh about running off the side of the road to wake up. This was back in the days when road rumbles consisted of natural obstacles like ditches, logs and mailboxes. Needless to say, this caused some concern for my mother. Daddy tried various methods of staying awake: snacking, playing the radio at 200 decibels, rolling the window down in the rain and so forth. Finally, one day Momma presented Daddy with an ear alarm. This was a little device that Daddy wore over his ear, and when he started to doze off and his head nodded forward, the ear alarm would buzz and wake him up. So the next week when Daddy got back home, Momma asked how the ear alarm worked.

"Fine. It worked fine," he said.

"It kept you awake?" Momma asked.

"Well, no, but it taught me to sleep with my head up."

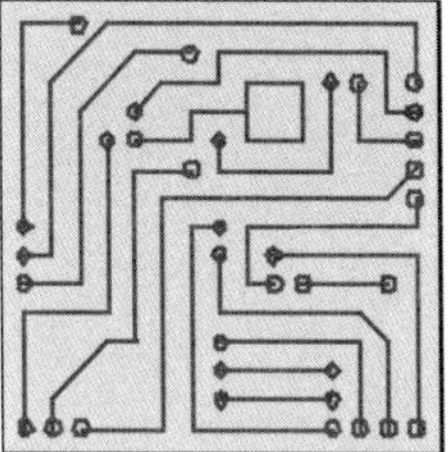

CHAPTER 32

When Campaigning Was Fun

My daddy ran for the House of Delegates twice. My mother ran for the House of Delegates once and for Congress once (notably, as the first woman from Virginia on a major party ticket). I ran for the House of Delegates once. Despite some close brushes with victory, the family record, so far, is 0-for-5. It is likely to stay that way. After watching the adolescent food fight that passed for a campaign this fall, I'm thinking, Why would anyone ever subject himself to that?

Campaigning is hard enough without having a pack of rabid squirrels leaping on your shoulders and accusing you of kicking Betty Sue in the shin in fifth grade.

What's really bad is the TV pundits pretend that is a more serious issue than, say, what the candidates propose to do about social security, illegal immigration and the threat from Islamo-fascism. "Now, Delores, are you concerned about damaging the self-esteem of young men in this country when you admit – although you have apologized millions and millions of times – that you once said boys have cooties?"

I'm waiting for the candidate who says, "So what? Boys DO have cooties!"

It's hard to believe, but campaigns used to be fun, sometimes even for the candidate. Yes, it's a lot of work and no sleep and you don't get to see your family for months and you gain a lot of weight on a diet in which pizza and cokes are the "healthy alternative." But there are the redeeming features of being criticized in public for your personal life, the exhilaration of accosting strangers with your campaign literature and the chance to plumb the depths of commitment that your spouse has to your marriage. All this is fun if you're a masochist; if you weren't, you wouldn't be running anyway.

I have numerous hilarious memories of being a candidate myself. Many of them involve chasing the school bus down Route 6 when Mrs. Owens (bless her heart) noticed that I was not at the corner to pick up six-year-old Katie Bo and refused to let her get off and stand on the side of the highway by herself. This happened many many times, because usually I was two counties away when school let out.

Being a candidate doesn't leave you much time for parenting, which, if done properly, is a time-intensive project. One morning late in the campaign when Katie Bo and I were both weary, she was reluctant about getting dressed and off to school. We engaged in lengthy negotiations that culminated in Katie's being dragged down the hall to Mrs. Starke's class by her grim-lipped, t-shirted, barefooted mother. I thought it was good that I got her there, almost on time, but the school administration was aghast.

Campaigning itself held daily surprises. One day a woman took one of my brochures, glanced at it and said, "You're running against him? I'll vote for you and I don't care what you stand for."

Not exactly the response I was expecting, but good enough.

Another time, a man approached me with his two young sons. He made a point of telling them to listen to what I said. This is surely a one-issue voter, I thought. I shook hands and awaited the question. Abortion? Minimum wage? Global warming? "Mrs. Williams," he began solemnly, "on Sunday, who are you for, Dallas or Washington?"

Fortunately, I was able to make a knowledgeable comment about the Redskins' quarterback, thus securing another vote.

Riding in parades is a big part of campaigning. We borrowed a convertible for one parade, but it rained and we had to put the top up. So I walked alongside the car with an umbrella, certain that people would think anybody walking in a thunderstorm with a metal rod in her hand was too dumb to vote for.

We tied balloons to the rearview mirror of the convertible for another parade. As we processed at a rather rapid pace, the balloons blew backwards, beating me in the face the whole way.

Finally, I gave up on the convertible and rode my horse in the next parade. But he was known to be frisky and I thought it would be bad if he kicked the offspring of any voters, so I drugged him heavily. However, he was so thoroughly tranquilized that he could hardly walk. Whenever a child ran out in the street to pick up candy, he swung his head around drunkenly as though to say, Wha' wuzzat?

Before I ran, my daddy gave me some sage advice, which, despite all the fun of my campaign, turned out to be right: "When you get to election day, you'll be so glad it's over you won't care whether you win or lose."

I'm sure a lot of candidates felt that way last Wednesday. I know the voters did.

CHAPTER 33

Feministas Hijack the Movies

Earlier this year, Betty Friedan died. She was the author of "The Feminine Mystique" and, although she wore lipstick, was one of the founding mothers of the feminist movement. A certain nationally-syndicated columnist who probably doesn't wear lipstick complained that Ms. Friedan did not get any thanks from conservative women with careers.

My guess is that, while conservative women appreciate the opportunity to work themselves into the ground, short-change their families and ruin their health, they're annoyed about what Ms. Friedan and her colleagues at the National Organization for Women have done to men.

There is a fixed amount of intelligence in the world, and now that women have most of it, guys are all buffoons. As women have become stronger and more self-reliant, men have been left with only a few tattered shreds of self-esteem.

We know this from watching the movies.

We see, for instance, that men have learned to get in touch with their feminine side – and forgotten how to fix cars, shoot guns and kick bad guys in the rear. Now they bumble around and watch women hot wire the Hummer, reload the AK-47 and kick bad guys in a sensitive part of their anatomy.

In the old days, leading men did not have to act like dimwits so that women could look strong and self-reliant. In "True Grit," 14-year-old Mattie Ross demonstrates her toughness by swimming her pony across the river. John Wayne, instead of breaking down on the riverbank in tears, watches proudly and says, "By God! She reminds me of me!"

Today, hot young guys in the movies have to cry to show what good actors they are. Think of Tom Cruise in "Mission Impossible: III," "Jerry McGuire," and almost anything else. And Ben Affleck ("Pearl Harbor," etc.) is a veritable waterworks. In the old days, even women didn't cry that much in the movies (except the ones in the audience).

Today, if they did a remake of "Casablanca" and they cast Mel Gibson in Humphrey Bogart's role as Rick, they'd have to rewrite the entire ending. Rick gives up the love of his life, Ilsa (Drew Barrymore), and, as the plane takes off in the fog, he breaks down, weeping, on the tarmac. Louie (Adam Sandler) helps the emotionally distraught Rick back to the bar where he spends the rest of his life a broken man in a lugubrious, alcoholic daze.

No need to rewrite the old James Bond movies to conform to the feminist ideal. The new one, "Casino Royale," already does that. After 33 years of Sean Connery-imposters defining Bond as a pillow-fluffing metrosexual, Daniel Craig supposedly reprises the original. But they should have cast the sobbing Orlando Bloom ("Elizabethtown") to play the new, kinder, gentler, tearful Bond. Sean Connery would be spinning in his grave, if he were dead.

Even anti-heroes Paul Newman and Robert Redford were never weepy wusses. Take "Butch Cassidy and the Sundance Kid." Remake with Matt Damon and Ben Affleck. The posse chases our heroes onto a rocky ledge above a shallow river. Damon says, "We gotta jump." Affleck refuses. They argue. Damon demands, "What's wrong with you?" Whereupon Affleck bursts into tears and blubbers out a heart-wrenching story about his stepmother trying to drown him in the bathtub. Damon chokes up, gives his buddy an emotional hug and urges him to seek counseling if they get out of this fix alive.

Betty Friedan's philosophical heirs would probably like to remake "Dirty Harry" with anybody but Clint Eastwood. Picture Jude Law holding a .44 magnum and saying, "I know what you're thinking: Did he fire six shots or only five?...You've got to ask yourself one question: Do I feel lucky?" The punk puts his hands over his face and begins sobbing. Jude kneels beside him, gently peels his hands away and says, "Let it out.

Let the healing begin."

It is probably sacrilegious even to suggest remaking "Gone with the Wind," with or without Clark Gable, but if James Bond can cry, Hollywood is capable of anything. In the NOW version, Hugh Grant would play Ashley, Vin Diesel would be Rhett and Susan Sarandon, Scarlett. As the mist swirls around their mansion, Rhett and Scarlett have their tension-filled farewell conversation.

Rhett/Diesel – I'm outta here.

Scarlett/Sarandon – What do you plan to use for money?

Rhett/Diesel – (short laugh) I made millions with Blockade Runners, Inc.

Scarlett/Sarandon – Oh Rhett, don't you know I bought up all the stock in B. R. Inc. with the money I made from my environmentally-friendly sawmill? You're in my debt.

Rhett/Diesel – (weeping) Where will I go? What will I do?

Scarlett/Sarandon – You will go straight to Savannah and begin restoring the wetlands for our coastal subsidiary.

Rhett/Diesel – Yes, dear. Anything else?

Scarlett/Sarandon – Oh, I'll think about that tomorrow.

Rhett/Diesel – (makes obeisance, withdraws) Hasta la vista, Madame Chairman.

CHAPTER 34

Untangling the Christmas Lights

There used to be a feature in one of the women's magazines of the '60s called "Can This Marriage Be Saved?" (The publication of this feature foreshadowed the invention of divorce in the 1970s.) In each issue, the reporter described a couple who had reached an impasse in their relationship. There was a long section from each partner describing the dreadful conditions under which he or she was living, followed by analysis and counseling from a professional marriage-fixer.

I have often thought of those articles when my husband, Cricket, and I were having an argument over whether to use 40-watt or 60-watt bulbs in the ceiling fan light, or whether or not the cat who purrs like a chain saw should be allowed to sleep in the bed, or some other relationship-threatening issue. We pause in the argument, each glaring at his bull-headed spouse, and suddenly the words come out, "Can this marriage be saved?" And we laugh.

Actually, after 26 years together, Cricket and I get along pretty well. We have each decided to pick our battles and stop sweating the small stuff. Cricket knows, for instance, that I have a hard time getting out the door to go anywhere, so, instead of nagging and hollering, he just sits down and reads the paper until I am standing outside with my coat on, saying, "Are you coming?"

And I have learned, for my part, that Cricket abhors cheap, particle board, some-assembly-required furniture, so I try not to buy more than one or two pieces a year.

One of the items that we have yet to settle, though, has to do with the Christmas tree. From start to finish, we disagree about the tree.

I have totally bought into the Norman Rockwell notion of the tree being the focal point for family warmth and togetherness during this holiest of holidays. I envision the three of us – Mom, Dad and little Katie Bo – roaming the snowy forest with an ax and a sled, seeking (and finding) the perfectly proportioned, nine-foot frasier fir. Dad chops the tree with a few well-aimed swings, and, accompanied by our frolicking dog, we pull it home on the sled. At home in front of the crackling fire with mugs of hot chocolate, we string the lights and all join in to hang the ornaments, remembering the history of each one in a jolly story.

Okay, so I live in a fantasy world.

To start with, the forests we have access to are all cedar or white pine. While fragrant, those species have long, droopy branches that will not support any of my collection of ceramic foxes. I know this from gluing the pieces back together.

Second, and more to the point, Cricket's romantic idea of harvesting the perfect tree involves driving by the Jaycees' lot on the way home from work.

This year at least he took me with him, and he even let me pick out the tree. So I'm thinking there's hope for our marriage. But as he went off to pay for it, he directed the helper to cut the bottom limbs off. I looked at the tree and foresaw the empty hole that would appear if the bottom limbs were severed, so I told the helper, "Just leave the limbs. We can cut them off later."

Of course, when we got home and Cricket tried to put the stand on the tree, he groused, "I thought I told that guy to cut the bottom limbs off."

Having been married 26 years and learned how to pick my battles, I merely nodded sympathetically. "Mmm-hmm."

Over the years, stringing the lights has proven to be the biggest area of contention. I think the lights should be laced loosely around the tree so that the tip of each branch twinkles. Cricket, in the name of structural integrity, would prefer to bind the trunk as snugly as possible so that the lights are embedded in the bark and cast shadows of the ornaments outward.

We find ourselves on opposite sides of the tree, standing on chairs, holding wads of tangled lights, arguing heatedly about aesthetics vs. physics in the hanging of Christmas lights. Finally, the voice of maturity interrupts and Katie Bo says, "Y'all stop arguing at Christmas."

Chastened, I agree to retire from the field of battle and let Cricket string the lights any blankety-blank way he pleases. When he's done, he calls me in to add the decorations, which I do without any help or interference from anyone else.

No crackling fire. No hot chocolate. No laughing family reminiscing about the ornaments. No Norman Rockwell.

Magazine reporter: Can this marriage be saved?

Marriage counselor: Only if the couple agrees to buy a pre-lit, artificial tree.

CHAPTER 35

The Bloody Christmas Photo

A few years ago, I told our friends from out of state that while I loved seeing the annual Christmas card picture of their children – and, indeed, I saved them in an album – I wanted to see the grownups, too. Unless they have a really good cosmetic surgeon, friends from 20 years ago have changed. And when your only contact with people is a card once a year, you have to glean clues about their lives from the family photo.

"Cousin Roy must be doing well. It looks like the picture was taken in Mexico – unless that's a backdrop at the J. C. Penney studio. And look, he's gotten a new wife. I wonder what happened to Gladys?"

One reason people tend to use a picture of the children is that it is hard to get the whole family together, hair combed, shirts buttoned, eyes open and mouths shut. Getting a family picture should not be as hard as it is. In fact, it would be a snap if everyone would just cooperate, but nooooo.

Some person complains that he's too busy replacing the belt on the lawn mower. Then other persons take their cue from Dad and sulk around, refusing to change clothes and making grimaces at the camera. Meanwhile, the Fun Director chirps cheerfully at the children and makes veiled threats through her teeth to the dad.

Having told our friends how to do their Christmas cards, I felt the bar was raised for our own card. It was my thought that, since we have only one child, we should include our pets to fill up all the empty space around the people. Katie Bo received this news with the same enthusiasm that children everywhere exhibit at the prospect of posing on command.

Cricket thought I was insane.

At the time, our pets numbered 11, more than half of which were cats. It would be a challenge, I knew, but since one of the cats was leash-broke, I thought we could pull it off.

We've done the photo with all the animals five or six times, and the results have been mixed. ("Mixed with blood," Cricket mutters.)

Arranging the animals is always a challenge. Beyond the mere idea of getting six cats, two dogs and three horses within 100 yards of each other, you have to take into account the relative size of the subjects. Cats are tiny next to horses. We learned that the first year when we had cats on leashes at our feet and horses leaning over the fence behind us. You could see the horses real well, but we had to put arrows on the photo to point out the cats.

The next year we tried holding the cats up in the air next to the horses' faces. That led to a lot of blood spilled without accomplishing the objective, because the dog was left on the ground alone. So the next year we put the dog on a table with a tablecloth. Then it looked like we were having a used pet sale.

Another problem we found the first year was that Cricket is not a good cat-holder. He holds a cat like it was a football, and we have only one cat who tolerates that. But even Kramer could tolerate only so much, and he began pulling himself onto Cricket's shoulder with his claws. Whereupon Cricket dropped the cat, who ran down in the woods. So we had to lock the rest of the cats in nearby cars, crates, the barn, etc., while I went down in the woods to retrieve Kramer.

For the next take, we had Cricket hold Carmen, who is like a stuffed animal who happens to be alive. As it turned out, there were limits to Carmen's good nature, too. After fetching Carmen from down in the woods, I suggested Cricket hold the horses and Katie Bo and I would handle the cats. Cricket got the horses lined up, Katie Bo had one cat in her arms and one on a leash, we had two in a crate and I had two in my arms.

All we had to do was get the dogs to join us. We called them and threw dog biscuits at the designated spot. Dixie Belle posed obligingly but Whiskey was afraid of the horses. So we ended up with three people, six cats, three horses and a dog huddled together in the driveway and then a lot of empty space off to the left with a dog lying there by herself.

Having run through several photographers over the years, last year I just made up a card with a separate shot of each member of the family. This year, feeling ambitious again, I am working on presenting the animals by species: one shot of the horses, one of the dog, one of the people. As usual, the cats provide the challenge.

But I have found that with a fast enough shutter speed and enough little crystal bowls of poached hummingbird tongues, you can get a herd of cats to suspend hostilities and smile for the birdie – for 1/500 of a second.

CHAPTER 36

New Year's Resolution: A Crafty Solution

Every so often I have an attack of artsy-craftiness, which always ends in – if not outright disaster – something short of triumph.

It all started with an article about clothes pin dolls that I read when I was 13. At the time, my big brother, Bo, whom I idolized, played high school football, so I dressed 35 clothes pin dolls in a facsimile of the school uniform and affixed a felt number to each doll's back. My idea was for Bo to take the dolls to school and give them to his teammates as a gift of adoration from me, something any 17-year-old boy would, of course, be happy to do.

Somehow my parents managed to head me off, averting the destruction of Bo's macho image without hurting my feelings too much.

Like the clothes pin doll episode, my artsy-crafty attacks are characterized by deranged hubris: I see something I like but can't afford, say, a $50,000 custom-made, 8x10 needlepoint rug with an intricate hunting design, and I think, "I could make that."

Then I do a little research, buy some raw materials and begin trying to replicate an item that some skilled artisan has spent a lifetime learning how to make.

After trial and error and many trips to the craft store, I occasionally get something passable made. But once I get the hang of it, I lose interest. By the time the attack passes, I have accumulated a cupboard full of materials for needlepointing or faux painting or making jewelry. Or painting okra.

The crafting bug has been in abeyance for some time, but recently it reared its ugly head.

My friend Claire Forbes, a jeweler, and several other real artisans were having a craft sale. I asked her if I could come sell my book, "Chivalry, Thy Name Is Bubba." She said the sale was for handmade crafts and since I had not personally glued the pages in my book, no. So I said, "How about if I bring some okra?" Caught off guard, Claire agreed.

I grow a lot of okra, mostly to eat, but also because I like how the overgrown pods look, dried and painted, in a tall vase. At that moment, we had about 75 stalks of okra drying on the sun porch, just in case we needed them. I had spray-painted some for the garden club sale, and I was going to paint some for Christmas gifts if I could keep my husband, Cricket, from throwing them away first.

But suddenly they were valuable! I became an okra painting factory. Silver. Gold. Copper. Pink. Teal. I sprayed okra in the basement, nearly asphyxiating the family. I sprayed okra in the driveway, leading to some interesting effects on the cars.

It takes a lot of paint to cover 75 stalks of okra, so I had to go to the craft store several times. Then I began buying vases, testing sizes and shapes, necessitating more trips to the craft store. There, the gorgeous spools of holiday ribbon seduced me, and I succumbed to a mad buying spree of accessories to go with unnaturally painted okra.

Eventually I began assembling the advertised "dried arrangements" and discovered that I needed something to hold the four-foot tall, top-heavy stalks in place. Marbles. Sand. Floral clay. Crinkle wrap. I was now making twice-daily pilgrimages to the craft store, 15 miles away.

Once I had the structural issues resolved, I decided the arrangements needed a little more oomph to qualify as handmade crafts, so I began experimenting with ribbon, excelsior, colored tissue and feathers to fill the vases.

By then the craft store had reserved a cash register exclusively for me.

Finally, I got a couple of arrangements put together and called Dotty Fevre to inspect my wares. She pronounced them sale-worthy. Then she got to fooling with the ribbon, making elaborate bows and asking where my glue gun was. Armed with her ideas and encouragement, I went back to the craft store, where they had named a wing in my honor.

All of this fevered activity occurred in the space of a week, during which I did not sleep or feed my family or speak in anything other than a testy, ominous voice. Cricket watched in amusement and waited for the disease to run its course.

My appointment with okra destiny finally arrived, and I couldn't get the blasted things in the car. Tall and fragile, structurally unsound, the dried okra arrangements could not be transported without specially-devised equipment, packing crates and padding. It took numerous trips to the show, because I could move only two at a time.

In the end, I did sell one. I even sold a few books, which was the point of the exercise.

Yesterday, sitting amongst festive vases of gold-painted okra, I told Cricket, "My new year's resolution is 'no more crafting.'"

"How about 'no more okra'?" he replied.

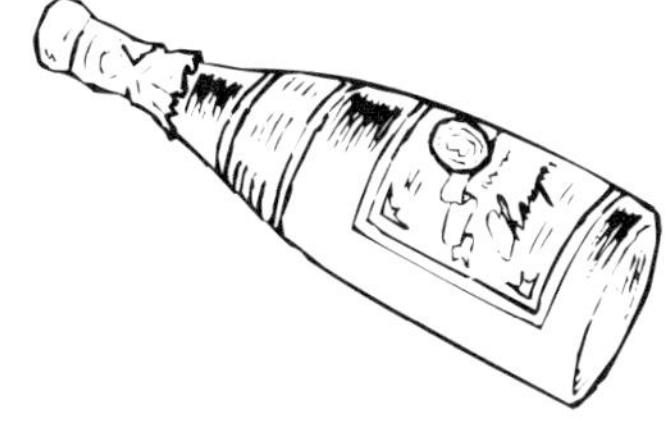

CHAPTER 37

Running on Pam Time

My friend Pam Ottley has so many responsibilities and distractions in her life that she can never predict accurately when she will arrive anywhere. Her loyal clients accept her tardiness with good humor. They call it "running on Pam time."

I, too, frequently find myself running on Pam time. As is the case with Pam, it is not my fault that I am late. The blame should be laid at the feet, paws and hooves of our animals and children.

Today, for instance, I was dressed to leave for a meeting when the guys who were going to paint the horse trailer drove up, unannounced. So I had to talk to them, discuss where to find a ball for the hitch that they forgot to bring, put on boots, move the horses, change back into my dress shoes – and leave ten minutes late.

This happens all the time, every time, in fact, that I am dressed up to go do something in my Professional Life. Often, I blow into a meeting room full of suits, five or ten minutes late, and all the men who have secretaries and wives to organize their paperwork and manage their pets and children look up to see that, as usual, Robin is the last one here. Despite the fact that I, too, have on a suit, I feel momentarily out of place. *You have no idea*, I think, looking around the table. *You have no idea about the secret life of Robin Williams. You think I am a suit-wearing professional meeting-goer who says things like "What are the Sarbanes-Oxley ramifications of this restatement of the 10Q?" If you only knew...*

Recently, we have been dog-sitting Carbon Copy, my mother's dog. He is a keeshond, a medium-sized, adorable but citified dog with 10-inch fur. Having a keeshond in the country is kind of like having a motorized dust mop: He goes out and sweeps up all the dirt, leaves, twigs, small rodents, etc. on the ground and then brings them inside. He's reminding us about the joys of living close to nature.

The first day we had him, I managed to get dressed and out the door to a meeting on time(!), but that was the last time. While I was out, Copy went on an unsupervised romp around all 2,500 acres of the State Farm next door, during which he collected globs of mud and, conservatively, 500 cockleburs. They were all over his legs (where the hair is only about six inches long), matted into his armpits, along his sides, between his legs, all up his chest. When I hosed him off and tried to pat him dry with a towel, the towel stuck to him like Velcro. We have pictures. Fortunately, we also have the dog, who was lost for two hours. After searching all of Crozier on horseback, our daughter, Katie Bo, finally found him frolicking in the briar patch.

So that night and for many more, I sat on the floor and combed burrs out of Copy's coat. The next morning, when I was leaving for a meeting, Copy rubbed up against me and ripped my stockings with the burrs, necessitating a delay while I changed, putting me, once again, on Pam time.

Sometimes it takes both pets and children to make me late.

At one time in my life, I chaired a state regulatory board, which met in an august courtroom downtown. There were serious issues involved in our work, and tempers often ran high among those addressing the board, so I had to appear dignified and authoritative to maintain control of the volatile meetings. It was a persona I put on with my suit.

Katie Bo never got sick except on the third Wednesday of the month, when I was supposed to chair the meetings. One memorable morning, I decided she was sandbagging me and we headed to school over her protests. Half way down Cardwell Road, she threw up in the car.

"I told you I was sick!" she wailed.

So: Take her home, put her to bed, get a neighbor to stay till the sitter could come, clean up the car. I had carefully laid my suit jacket across the back seat before leaving home, but I had left the car door open when I helped the sick child get out, so when I went back to clean up the car -- and hopefully leave for downtown -- I found the dog in the back seat lying on my jacket.

The meeting definitely ran on Pam time that month.

CHAPTER 38

Copy's Excellent Adventure, Part II

We have a little mud puddle that we dignify with the word "pond." It's fed by the runoff from a hill and about every third winter it gets enough ice to skate on. Tuesday it was 10 degrees. Wednesday, when it was a balmy 22, I went down to check the ice.

The dogs obligingly tested it first, walking gingerly on the shallow end. Gyp, the country dog, retreated when the ice cracked, but our citified and heavy-coated visitor, Copy, was having so much fun skittering on the ice that he decided to take off at full speed across the pond. I watched the entire surface of the ice wave in his wake before his 45 pounds made a big hole in the middle of the deep end.

Copy, in great surprise, began paddling vigorously – only to find himself hemmed in. Although the ice broke every time he pawed it, he kept changing direction. He was making the hole bigger but making little progress towards the bank. I ran to the dam and called him. Thinking the other side might be closer, I ran to another point. Then I came back to the dam. The dog was still paddling frantically in all directions.

By now the dog had been in the water three or four minutes. How long could he last? There was the strength issue, the shock of the cold water, the toll of his struggles with the wet weight of his massive fur coat. We had no boat, no dock. There was no branch long enough to reach 20 feet out to the ice hole. Even if I had time to go for help, what help would I go for?

As I watched, Copy got a grip on the edge of the ice and hung on, catching his breath. He looked pathetic and desperate.

Oh man. I didn't want to go in the water. I remembered one time, years ago, North Pole owner Harvey Layne telling me about a cow falling through the ice. Harvey, then about 75 years old, stripped down, took a rope and went in after her. Both of them survived.

There seemed nothing to do but wade in and get the dog. I had a fleeting moment of hesitation as I imagined stepping in the mucky muddy pond bottom. I kept my duck boots on in fear of snapping turtles, and I kept my goose down jacket on because I didn't want to be cold.

Okay, sometimes in emergencies, people don't think rationally.

Several years ago, we had the pond renovated. The trees growing on the dam were removed, the pond dredged and the dam raised, so that the former mud puddle was now actually deep enough to drown in.

I wasn't sure exactly how deep it was, but I learned pretty quickly. It fell off as soon as I waded through the cattails. In no time, I was slogging through gooshy pond muck with water up to my neck.

Really glad I had on those boots. And the jacket.

The dog was once again paddling frantically in all directions. I could hear myself calling him in a hoarse voice. The cold water had taken my breath away. I hoped it wouldn't take my pulse away.

When I was in five feet of water, Copy was still a couple or three yards away, so I plunged ahead, kicking with my legs and breaking the ice as I swam towards him.

Readers of this column will remember from Copy's Excellent Adventure, Part I, wherein the city dog romped around the State Farm collecting cockleburs, that Copy is a keeshond with 10-inch fur. As I was thrashing around among the ice floes of Pond Williams trying to rescue the dog, I was glad he had a coat like a lion's mane to grab onto.

I suppose, once I had broken a path, the dog would have paddled to safety on his own. But I decided not to wait and see. I grabbed his scruff with my right hand, took what seemed like 87 strokes with my left arm and got us back to where I could touch bottom.

At that point, the gooshy pond muck under my feet felt pretty good.

I shoved Copy through the cattails to where he could touch bottom, and we clambered up the steep bank, our coats heavy with ice water.

As we climbed the hill to the house, I couldn't help thinking, *This would be a good time for a hot flash.* Copy undoubtedly felt the same way, because by the time we got to the back door, his coat was a mass of icicles. He did something he's probably never done before: shivered.

All I could think was, it's a good thing this didn't happen the day before, when it was *really* cold.

CHAPTER 39

You're Never Too Old to Be Carded

A childhood friend of mine was giving me an update on her life, telling me how young and energetic she felt, and she said, "You know, 50 is the new 35, so I must be about 38 years old."

That's all well and good, as my husband, Cricket, would say, but how many Fountain of Youth drugs and devices does it take to facilitate that fantasy? (Levitra, Bowflex, Rograine, Jenny Craig, Just for Men, Centrum Silver, Red Bull, etc.)

Nevertheless, there must be something to what my friend says, because people really are living longer. We know this because the greeting card industry has begun selling cards for people reaching their 100th birthday. And there are several choices! You would expect a couple of choices for 80th and maybe even 90th, but apparently there's enough of a market for 100th birthday cards that the store has a selection to choose from (depending on whether the recipient is still going strong or just hanging on by a thread).

Of course, the wording for them is somewhat different from that of other cards, just as the wording on cards for 21st and 50th birthdays is different, based on what the honoree is likely doing at that stage in his life. In fact, a perusal of the birthday card rack gives a quick view of life's stages.

Sometimes the wording of a card reflects the wishful thinking of the sender. This is famously true of cards for "sweet 16"-year-olds, which always imply a level of innocence teenagers haven't enjoyed since "The OC" replaced "Full House" as the must-see TV show.

Of all the ages, 21 is the only one with an immutable image. In a society that does everything possible to retard adulthood for young people and then promotes an artificial return to youth by everyone over 40, 21 nevertheless remains the symbolic dividing line. Thus, birthday cards for people turning 21 always focus on their legal maturity, something that may or may not coincide with their maturity regarding adult beverages (or anything else).

Twenty-one may be a milestone, but the real dividing line between youth and maturity is the big 3-0, something that is confirmed by the crepe-draped cards. The message in 30th birthday cards is, you're really an adult now because people call you "Sir."

Fortunately, though, society does not expect you to remain an adult for long. In the old days, having your 40th birthday meant you had crossed the threshold into middle age, a time when you took up pipe smoking, combing your thinning hair over and calling men in their 30s, "young man," as in "Young man, when I was your age…" But now 40 is the age of starting over, as people are starting their second marriages and second families. So the cards crack wise with sex jokes.

Consistent with the backward spinning of the clock established at 40, cards for 50-year-olds reflect their youthful activities. At his 50th birthday, the weekend warrior needs a get-well card for his football-related injuries. When 50 was just 50, women got cards punning hot flashes; now they get cards extolling what hot babes they are. The "over-the-hill" comments that used to appear on cards for 40- and 50-year-olds have now migrated to the 60- and 70-year-old section. "Hill? What hill? I didn't see any hill!" is the bold attitude of the 50-year-old, who plans to celebrate by bungee-jumping from a helicopter over the Hoover Dam.

Fifty may well be the new 35, but 60- and 70-year-olds inexorably suffer the indignities of aging, and their cards reflect that reality, with many references to forgetfulness, false teeth and incontinence, sometimes all at once. Nevertheless, the expectation is that the honoree will celebrate vigorously, despite the prospect of suffering for it later.

A tone of respect, heretofore absent, begins to creep into the cards for the 80s. The typical card salutes the honoree for exceeding his biblical allotment of three score and ten and suggests a quiet gathering of family and any friends still alive and lucid. Some cards boldly wish the recipient many happy returns for the coming year.

For the 90s, card writers, awed by the fact the recipients were born A Long Time Ago and fearful of jinxing anything, tactfully avoid drawing attention to the coming year. Instead, they speak of warming one's self with memories of friends and family, a subtle shift from expectations for the future to a recognition that you probably get your pleasure from living in the past, if you can remember it.

By the time you get to 100, the cards, far from encouraging a raucous celebration, are just expressing hope that you will get through the day without medical intervention.

"And many happy returns for the coming five minutes."

I thought the cards would say, "Boogie on! 100 is the new 70!"

CHAPTER 40

Is Your Car on Fire?

We used to laugh about tire fires, not because we are indifferent to environmental disasters, but because the people associated with one, when interviewed on television, invariably referred to the event as a "tar far." But tar fars seem less amusing now that we have been through a couple of car fars.

The first conflagration occurred in our driveway. I had run up to the post office in Cricket's car and on the way home, I noticed a thin string of smoke emanating from the dash panel. I thought through my options carefully and made all the wrong decisions.

It was an electrical fire, and I should have shut the engine off immediately, if not sooner. But I didn't want to inconvenience the neighbors with a burned-out hulk blocking the road, so I drove a few hundred yards to our driveway. I didn't want to block our driveway, either, so I drove further, to a nice place where I could pull off, yet still be on the gravel, away from trees, easily accessible for fire trucks, convenient for spectators, and so forth.

While I was riding around looking for a suitable place for a car fire, the thin string of smoke became a lung-choking cloud filling the front seat. Seven-year-old Katie Bo was crying, "Mom! Stop the car! Let me out!"

When I stopped, she and the dog jumped out and ran to the house. I gathered the mail, the car phone, my purse, keys, tissue box, etc., and went to call the fire department. You can practically see the fire department from our house, so a bunch of volunteer firemen with two trucks and an impressive amount of gear showed up in about three minutes.

I barely had time to get my camera and take pictures of Cricket's

Blazer, which was, in fire department lingo, "fully engaged." Flames were shooting up 20 or 30 feet, and the tires were popping one by one. When it was over, Katie and I inspected the little heap of charred remains. I was thinking, Wow, there's not much metal in a car these days, when Katie said, "Mom, do you think my favorite stick is still in there?"

We later framed the photo with the caption: "Blaze of Glory."

Two years later I was driving my van to the beach. The interstate was crowded but rolling. Suddenly, the engine cut off and Katie saw a thin string of smoke emanating from the dash panel. She called it to my attention, helpfully adding her interpretation. "The car's on fire!"

Being older and wiser, I contradicted her, because nobody has two cars burn up under her. We coasted along at 65 mph for a few seconds while I pondered the phenomenon. Meanwhile, nine-year-old Katie Bo was crying, "Mom! Stop the car! Let me out!"

For whatever reason, the engine was off, so I had to pull over. Katie leaped out and ran to the trees. As the smoke increased, I began to think she was right: the car was on fire. With trembling hands, I hooked leashes on the two dogs. Katie held them, and I went back to the side of the van and began heaving clothes, bags, towels, groceries and stuff in the ditch with both hands.

The fire truck came promptly but the car burned up anyway. I have pictures of that one, too. The state police came, but they left soon to deal with all the fender-benders caused by people slowing down to look at the fire.

I called Cricket and got his voice mail. He saved it for me: "Cricket," my voice says loudly but calmly against the background of interstate traffic, "you won't believe this. I'm standing here watching… (voice breaking) my car burn up."

Katie Bo and I were sitting on the side of the road with our bundles like refugees when the wrecker arrived. The operator winched the car onto the bed of his truck, but he didn't lower it all the way. "Six months ago I picked one up after a car far," he said, "and when I drove off, the wind kicked the far up again. Burned the whole back of my truck. So now I leave 'em tilted. If it catches again, I'll cut it loose."

Following her extensive first-hand experience, Katie Bo wrote a manual titled "Is My Car Burning Up?" Chapter One describes how to tell when your car is on fire. "The engine may cut off. This doesn't happen in all cases, but that is a very good sign you have a car problem."

Chapter Two is called "What to do and when to do it." The gist of that chapter seems to be "JUST PULL OVER!"

Thanks to Katie Bo, next time, I'll be prepared.

CHAPTER 41

Dating 101 – Rule #1

When our daughter, Katie, started dating, I did what the women in our family have done for generations: I taught her how to play The Game.

The Game is a system of rules that help girls deal with guys. The rules are constructed on the notion that girls want affection and security and guys want sex. My grandmother summarized the girls' rules this way: Pull him towards you with one hand and push him away with the other.

If you don't think the system works, consider Anne Boleyn. She played The Game superbly with Henry VIII. He blew off the Pope, created a new state religion and divorced the queen so he could marry her. (Anne lost her touch later on, but in the beginning she was really good.)

I began by giving Katie a word of caution: Don't trust your girlfriends. This was hard for her to believe because she had lots of girlfriends. But I warned her not to say anything about her love life unless she wanted the information posted on the school bulletin board.

Talk to me, talk to your cousin, talk to somebody from another high school -- in another state, preferably – but don't talk boys to any girl who goes to your school.

Then I told her the first rule of The Game: Girls do not call boys. This, also, was hard for her to believe because every girl she knew called boys regularly, emailed them, texted them, chased them down the halls, lay in wait for them outside the locker room and hounded them 'most to death.

What was confusing was that it seemed to work. The loudest, meanest, most insecure middle school girls each had some poor pimply-faced boy locked in a half-nelson.

I explained to Katie how unsatisfying it was for a girl to chase a boy. Even if she caught him, she couldn't relax. Boys who are trapped are apt to bolt. Better for him to chase you.

Girls today are no different from girls of yore in that they want to acquire the status symbol of dating. It's just that the status symbol of yore was to have lots of beaux, whereas the status symbol today is to have a boyfriend.

Having a boyfriend is more important than clear skin, blond hair or hot shoes. The need for a BF is so strong that it overrides any sense of dignity or self-respect.

If the boy is not attentive, it doesn't matter; the girl calls, e-mails, IMs, sends text-messages, drives over to his house, moves into the basement, does his homework, appeals to his mother, writes things on his family's calendar, whatever it takes to keep him engaged in the relationship. Guilt is as good as love. Inertia is too.

Should the boy somehow summon the courage to tell her he is breaking up with her, he will be subjected to a flood of attention including two-hour cell phone sessions in the middle of the night during which the girl cries and threatens suicide.

As a friend of mine -- the mother of two boys who are besieged by girls -- says, "Why are girls today so needy?" Why, indeed? It's ironic that the daughters of the women's liberation generation don't have enough self-confidence to say, I'm special, he'll have to chase *me*.

Recently a smart, self-possessed young lady asked me for dating advice. She and her boyfriend were at different colleges, and, I gathered, the long-distance romance was not going well. "I always had to do the calling," she said, "so one day I decided not to call him until he called me first."

After two weeks, she still had not heard from him. Her parents thought she should call him and find out what was going on. Her inclination was not to. I didn't come right out and say, Sweetie, you *have* no boyfriend, but I did applaud her restraint. "You've got too much on the ball to chase after some boy and beg for his attention," I told her.

That was when I realized it's the mothers who are clueless. When I was instructing Katie in The Game, I always assumed other mothers were doing the same thing (despite abundant evidence to the contrary). But no.

One of the many unfortunate by-products of the Sixties was the creation of a whole generation of girls who never learned how to play The Game. This meant their daughters had no one to learn from.

Girls are making fools of themselves chasing boys because they don't know any better. They need someone to tell them how to play The Game.

Okay, I will.

Rule #1: Girls Do Not Call Boys.

There are further refinements to The Game, but they all proceed from Rule #1.

CHAPTER 42

Dating 202 – "Call Me"

The response to my column, Dating 101, has been huge. In fact, I haven't gotten so much feedback since I wrote an article for a Major Metropolitan Daily in which I poked gentle fun at kids playing T-ball. For awhile there I thought the parents were going to torch my house and carry my head off on a pike.

In Dating 101, I advanced the bold idea that girls should not call boys. This idea was met with disbelief, derision and amusement. That was the mothers.

Girls themselves were doubtful but interested in hearing more, mainly, How do we get the boys to call us?

They have to be told, of course. You say, "Call me."

Just because a girl shouldn't make the call herself doesn't mean she can't tell a boy she wants to hear from him.

Boys and girls send each other signals of their interest all the time. Boys send out signals to see if it's okay to come closer. Girls send signals telling boys to pursue them – or not. But it's been so long since anybody has played The Game that the receptors are rusty. Girls are so busy doing the talking they don't pick up the signals the boys are sending.

At some point, girls decided it was too much trouble to send all these coded signals indicating their receptivity to male attention, and they started calling boys, emailing boys, calf-roping boys and otherwise announcing their interest in them. This took all the fun out of The Game for boys, who thrive on competition. So the typical boy turned instead to Wii, occasionally setting the joystick down long enough to put the phone on speaker so some girl could tell him how cute he was.

Resolving this problem will take perseverance. Boys are basically lazy, but they can be trained.

For years, nay, for almost two generations, girls have trained boys to let them, the girls, do all the work in a relationship. It hasn't been hard. Boys may be lazy but they are no fools. What guy would not be willing to hang around the house and wait for a girl to drive herself over, bring the beer, do his laundry, clean the mold out of the refrigerator and buy her own ticket to the concert?

When girls stop doing all the work, boys will be forced to take some initiative themselves -- or else live like monks, which, trust me, is not what boys will choose to do.

Of course, it has been so long since boys have been expected to pursue girls, it will take a little direction from the girls to get them started. Fortunately, this isn't hard, either. Guys of all ages appreciate having clear instructions about a girl's expectations.

Here's how it works: When you meet a guy and the sparks are flying, don't whip out your cell phone and ask for his number. Wait for him to ask for yours. If he doesn't, you smile brightly and say, "Give me a call some time."

Admittedly, this may sound like a novel idea to the guy, so you will have to repeat the instructions clearly as you part company: "Call me."

You say this lightly, because to be serious is to set yourself up for humiliation. Guys are, well, heartless when it comes to joking about girls. (They're heartless when it comes to joking about other guys, too, even their best friends.)

You must do a balancing act, simultaneously convincing the guy that you are wild about him and that you couldn't care less. "Pull him to you with one hand and push him away with the other," my grandmother always said. You tell him to call you, signaling your interest in him, but you use an offhand tone of voice, signaling that it wouldn't make any difference to you if he didn't.

All of this requires a little practice, which is what high school is for. As hard as it is for teenagers to believe, high school is not the peak experience of most people's lives. It's a time to practice dating skills with other people who are learning, too.

Everybody is more worried about himself than about you, so it doesn't matter if you don't get it exactly right the first time. Practice your dating skills now, with guys you aren't in love with, so that when you grow up and meet someone you really care about, you'll know how to manage the relationship.

For instance, if you meet Mr. Right and HE says, "Give me a call," just smile sweetly and apologetically and say, "I don't call boys. They call me."

This is the sort of thing that makes men crazy. Crazy about you, if you play The Game right.

CHAPTER 43

Pearls of Wisdom

Recently, we saw a darling little friend of ours, Meredith Thomas, at a party. She had on a lovely ensemble and a string of pearls. What a wise young lady, I thought.

"Always wear pearls," I told her. "They'll keep you out of jail."

I know this from first hand experience.

Some years ago when I was working for a Major Metropolitan Daily, I had occasion to write a series of articles about cocaine use in the metropolis. My editor thought this would be a great idea because I had just written a much-talked-about article on marijuana. The assignment bored me, initially, because the challenge of getting people to talk to me about their illegal drug use was pretty much the same.

However, the fact that cocaine use, possession and sale-of are much more serious legal offenses – felonies with heavy fines and prison time – quickly changed the dynamic.

No sooner did the series appear but a subpoena also appeared. Judge W cordially invited me to an intimate gathering of my peers in his chamber for the purpose of revealing who my confidential sources were.

I told him I would be happy to come to the festivities, but, as scummy as my sources were, I couldn't rat on them.

He was disappointed, naturally. He offered me certain inducements, such as being allowed to walk around freely for two weeks with a daily fine, before threatening more serious consequences.

I remember my two-week reprieve from jail mostly for the gallows humor. While Cricket and I sat on the porch with cocktails every night making jailhouse jokes, the city was, apparently, rampant with speculation.

Will she talk? Who were her sources?

Many people in the community offered their support in touching and amusing ways. A printer offered to make personal stationery for me with a pencil sketch of the city jail on the front. An artist offered to decorate my cell walls. Numerous people offered to contribute to my legal defense fund. Someone made up bumper stickers that said, "I don't use cocaine and I don't even know Robin Traywick."

Some of the people I had interviewed sent word of their support for my courageous silence. One offered inducements of a different sort for me to keep mum.

Here I should say that I really can't tell the whole story until a lot of people are dead, hopefully from natural causes.

It was a bizarre situation, one I never dreamed I would find myself in. Here's little ol' preppie Robin talking to felonious druggies and facing heavy fines and jail time of her own – and the guys in the news department were sick with jealousy. All of the hard-bitten City Desk reporters who covered crime and depravity daily were wondering how this chick in the features department (formerly, "The Women's Page") got all the glory of being a martyr for the First Amendment. I was wondering that, too, and also wondering how I could arrange for one of them to be the martyr.

While I was waiting to return to court, my lawyer, Sandy Wellford, and my husband, Cricket, were each doing their utmost to keep me out of the pokey. Sandy was doing the usual lawyerly thing -- and doing it especially well. Meanwhile, unbeknownst to anybody, Cricket did a very un-lawyerly thing. He called on the judge, whom he knew in another capacity, at home. He was not armed.

My by-line in the paper did not reflect my recent marriage to Cricket, and the judge was surprised to learn of this connection. Beyond that, as far as I know, they talked about the weather.

Throughout this ordeal, I was interested in how the newspaper would cover the trial of one of their own. First of all, they played it on the front page, tastefully below the fold. They ran a picture of me, and, I noted with curiosity, it was not the most recent picture the newspaper morgue had available. Since I had just had a new photo made, one that I thought made me look like Brenda Starr, Girl Reporter, I stopped by the morgue to ask about the substitution.

The staff there were deeply engaged in my legal dilemma, it turned out. "Oh," the head librarian said, "we used that one because you were wearing pearls. We decided they couldn't put anybody in jail who wore pearls."

Turns out they were right. On my return visit to court, there were several scary twists, but at the end of the day, older, wiser, with many prematurely gray hairs, I walked out of the building free.

All this time I've let Sandy Wellford and Cricket each think he kept me out of jail, but really, you know, it was the pearls.

CHAPTER 44

Is This Covered by Medicare?

It's been 12 years since I've had either a small child or a dog that wasn't a Labrador retriever, so the whole concept of "picky eater" has slipped my mind. It seems like such a ridiculous notion that I was surprised recently to hear my friend Jack talk about the difficulties they were having getting their dog to eat.

A dog? I thought. They can't get a dog to eat?

It seems their old dog had died and the young dog was in mourning. They had tried canned food, tempting him with luscious servings of beef 'n gravy or turkey giblets au jus and begging him sweetly to eat. The dog merely watched them sorrowfully.

Finally, Jack's wife found an article that said they had to convince the dog the food came from them, that is, they had to get their scent mingled with the food. So, Jack said, his wife began fondling the kibble and kneading the canned food with her hands.

It worked. The dog began to eat again.

Well, that's just silly, I thought, while driving my cat to the acupuncture vet.

We have an adorable, fluffy calico cat named Carmen who has an unattractive condition called irritable bowel syndrome. After trying various medications and putting her on a diet of prescription food that costs more than a flight on the space shuttle, we achieved only slight relief.

Carmen's condition was starting to tell on our marriage, so, having become really really desperate, I took her to Allison Faber, a vet who does acupuncture on cats – which is *way* more reasonable-sounding than kneading canned food for your dog.

First, she gave Carmen a chiropractic adjustment of her spine, which, apparently, was out of alignment. Then she stuck little needles in a double row down her spine. Carmen was outfitted with a miniature lampshade around her neck for this procedure.

To enhance the effect of the acupuncture, Carmen received B-12 injections. Finally, Allison said, "I'm going to order some Chinese herbs for Carmen."

"Naturally," I said and wrote a check.

It was hard to say who was more amazed at this experience, Carmen or I. Carmen took to her bed (our bed, actually) for 24 hours. Meanwhile, I described the treatment to my husband, who wanted to know if the next step was alternative medicine in Mexico.

Mexico was not an issue, because Allison's treatment worked. Carmen was cured! At least for a couple of weeks. Allison had warned me it would take several treatments to get to a maintenance level. Meanwhile, the Chinese herbs arrived. I had expected something like catnip, but the magical herbs had been ground into a fine brown powder with a strong odor. "Mix them with canned food," Allison suggested.

Thus, I embarked on a mission to get Carmen to eat Chinese herbs, a challenge that made Jack and his dog pale by comparison.

Like Jack, I tried luscious-sounding flavors of pet food: gourmet salmon mousse, lobster truffles au gratin, shrimp uber-schnitzel a la mode. Instead of 12 times a day, I fed Carmen only twice a day so she'd be good and hungry. Every morning I made a little mound of hearts of tuna foie gras on a crystal coaster, shook a gram of Chinese herbs over it, said the magic incantation, stirred it up and set it before the ravenous cat.

Of course, she wasn't *that* ravenous. After a week of this, I remembered Jack's dog. The next morning, when I was alone, I patted and squeezed the canned food to get my scent all over it.

I'm sure it was just a coincidence, but Carmen ate her breakfast that morning.

Carmen still got her prescription food at night, and she was doing quite well until I became overconfident.

I was trying to save money because the prescription food is so expensive, and, of course, I can't tell the other three cats not to eat it. I used to feed the barn cat Friskies, Carmen' favorite, but once Carmen found that out, I had to put prescription food at the barn, too. The barn cat is very generous about sharing her food with a stray tom and a 'possum. They may have rabies, mange and worms, but they don't have irritable bowel syndrome.

Our four cats, the stray and the 'possum were going through a bag of prescription food every week, so I bought a bag of "Special Care for Sensitive Systems" at the grocery store. I figured if Carmen could eat canned food, surely she could eat "Special Care for Sensitive Systems" food that cost five times what Friskies cost.

Wrong. Major relapse. More needles and lampshades. So okay, I'll keep buying her platinum-encrusted hummingbird tongues, forget the grocery store chow.

And Jack, I'm sorry I laughed at you.

CHAPTER 45

County's Getting Citified

The other day while I was stopped on Cardwell Road, waiting for Kitt Bosse's guineas to wander across the road, I got to thinking how the county was becoming too citified. This is a phenomenon that my husband, Cricket, has remarked on for some time. Fifteen years ago, when it got to where we didn't know everyone in the North Pole restaurant on any given night, Cricket said, "It's getting too crowded. We've got to move west."

I've lost track of the stoplights. Five? And new developments down every little road. Chain stores. *Two* liquor stores. Even an Internet café. Next thing you know, we'll have a mall.

My buddy Buck Fevre and I were lamenting recently about how, as soon as city folks move to the country, they set about making the rural life less rural. "Wonder whether it's living in the country, or just the idea of living in the country that's attractive to city folks," he mused.

My guess is that city folks like the country as long as it is part of the distant scenery, but when the realities of country life impact them personally…well, that's a different story.

We have a horsey county, and people seem attracted to the *idea* of living in an equestrian community. But I'm a little worried that one of them, while jogging on the bridle paths, will get the idea that horseback riders should carry a baggie to scoop up after their horses.

City folks seem surprised to find that people like to play outdoors in the country. Shooting sports are popular, but city folks, perhaps reminded of the shooting sports in certain undesirable sections of the city, don't want to hear "bang bang."

Nor do they want to hear barking dogs, log splitters or loud engines on pickup trucks and four-wheelers.

The surest sign rural life is threatened is when people start asking the supervisors to curtail farming activities. Fertilizing fields is offensive to urban noses.

Goochland County has been under pressure from the urban element for some time, but the definitive surrender of the country boys to the urban come-heres came last week when the supervisors enacted an emergency regulation banning mud-bogging.

Mud-bogging, for the uninitiated, is a competition that involves driving a vehicle into a giant mud hole at a high rate of speed. It is the sort of leisure activity that differentiates us from, say, New Yorkers. Out here in the country, we can make a sport out of anything.

What starts as a friendly afternoon of slogging through random mud holes often takes a competitive turn as the drivers, in true guy fashion, demand deeper mud and longer bogs. This gives them an excuse to get out the bulldozer. It also gives them an excuse to modify their trucks. Bigger tires. Higher lifts. And finally, re-routing the exhaust system so that it sprouts through the hood, enabling the vehicle to be virtually submerged without conking out.

Then it becomes necessary to improvise some kind of truck retrieval system. The solution is to hook a chain to the frame of the truck, so that when it gets stuck, it can be winched out.

Mud bogging is a fabulous spectator sport. A contestant drives to the starting line at the lip of the pit. There he sits, gunning the engine and letting the crowd admire his custom-painted, polished, jack-up truck. Suddenly, there is the roar of 400 horses as the gladiator charges into battle. Then there is the satisfying splat as he hits the muck, slopping waves of mud beyond the pit onto the spectators in the lower seats.

The crowd screams and whistles encouragement as the truck fishtails and grinds its way forward before emerging triumphantly on the other side -- or bogging down in the middle and being dragging ignominiously backwards by a tractor.

What a quintessentially American sport – combining fresh air, mud, roaring engines, modified trucks and the age-old challenge of man against nature.

Is this a great country, or what?

And yet we find distinctly un-American forces at work, right here in our back yard. There are people who would *ban* mud bogging. They want to tell you you can't invite a few friends over and drive your truck through a mud hole on your own property. They object to the noise and the mud that ends up on the public roads, as though this were the Fan District or Windsor Farms, where everyone is too refined for that sort of thing.

If this ban is made permanent on the 17th, then you can kiss country life goodbye. Hunting, fishing, farming, all will be outlawed. Owning more than one dog. Keeping cats in the barn. Keeping horses in the barn. Shooting ground hogs. Working on your own car. Playing in the dirt. Burning leaves. Skinny-dipping in the river.

Mark my words. This will be the end of uncivilization as we know it.

CHAPTER 46

KGR: Keeping Goochland Rural

As officials review the countywide land use plan, they wrestle with how to Keep Goochland Rural. At a recent public meeting, my husband asked, "Can we build a moat?" This is the approach favored by many.

If rural life simply meant fewer people, we could pull up the drawbridge. But rural life is also a state of mind – and not one that everybody in the county shares.

The rural state of mind stems from having a sparse population, open land and more room to do stuff, but that's not the whole picture.

Rural areas are characterized by private property and respect for the landowners. With more breathing room, people in rural areas seem to have less need for the government to regulate their affairs. There's more leeway for kids to run loose, pets to accumulate, engines to roar, grass to grow a little longer.

People know their neighbors but respect their privacy. They offer discreet help if there seems to be a problem. If the accumulation of weeds or pets or party guests or non-ambulatory vehicles becomes a nuisance, most people try neighborly communication first.

But as people increasingly demand that government solve their interpersonal problems instead of working out reasonable accommodations among themselves, it seems the rural state of mind is in danger of disappearing.

If Cricket and I were so inclined, we could complain about bio-sludge just upwind of our house or cattle that occasionally wander onto our property. We could complain about hunters in the fall or the shooting range that sounds like a Rambo movie marathon. We could complain about dogs barking and chasing our cats.

But: When the farms are gone, the rural countryside will be, too. The shooting range is part of a huge complex that will stay undeveloped as long as it is useful. Hunters promote game conservation as well as good stewardship of the land – the rural land we share. If we complain of other dogs, we'll get a leash law restricting our dogs, too.

Keeping Goochland Rural, then, would seem to mean retaining a certain attitude of tolerance, coupled with respect for the neighbors.

But how do we maintain the undeveloped land and spread-out feeling that fosters this state of mind?

The difficult part of KGR – the part that is seldom discussed – is that there has to be an economic reason to maintain land in an undeveloped state. Some of the things that make GR – the river, the wildlife, the scenery – belong to everyone. But what underpins those rural features is undeveloped land, which belongs to private owners.

How do you square "everybody's" desire to Keep Goochland Rural with each landowner's need to Keep Goochland Affordable? Landowners will leave their property undeveloped only as long as it makes economic sense.

Most people who own land in the country enjoy the openness themselves and do not want to develop it. But it is hard to justify paying money -- taxes -- to own property when you could receive large sums of money to sell it.

One way that "everybody" can enjoy the large tracts of undeveloped land that belong to individual landowners is for "everybody" – through the government – to buy the development rights. This works but it is expensive and often involves raising taxes on "everybody." It is only fair, of course, for "everybody" who wants to KGR to pay for it.

Another way to slow development is for landowners to find a low-impact use for their property. This means encouraging traditional activities such as crop farming, animal husbandry and forestry. In Goochland, the commercial management of horses, cattle, hay and timber have been the greatest contributors to the enduring rural atmosphere. But there are thousands of acres here lying fallow, ready to sprout rooftops.

As our urban areas grow, there is a demand for the rural experience, creating an opportunity for landowners to make use of their property without planting a row of houses. Landowners can establish private parks, in essence. There exist in many places such privately owned rural playgrounds as: fox pens, nature preserves, golf courses, recreational boating facilities, fishing areas, hunting preserves, 4x4 off-road courses and ranges for shooting sports.

"Everybody" who wants to KGR should support these and other creative uses of undeveloped land. This is a bigger issue than "I can do what I damn well please on my own property." The issue here is, Who's going to pay to Keep Goochland Rural? KGR is, in reality, a plea for the economic environment to maintain large undeveloped tracts of land.

So, as the county fathers ponder the land-use plan, we must all consider this question: Would you rather have a rural playground or farm next door – or a subdivision with the attendant traffic and taxes for more schools?

CHAPTER 47

When Cars Are Smarter Than People

Life in the electronic age is hard enough, what with VCRs to program and clocks to reset when the power blinks and cordless phones to retrieve from under the cushions. Who wants to have to outwit your own car just to drive to the post office?

I have a wonderful new car that I love. It's a Toyota Matrix and it gets 30 miles to the gallon, plus it is a stick shift and fun to drive. I have down-sized from a mini-van, since I don't have to haul children around any more. I do haul a lot of cargo around, still, and I was delighted to find that the Matrix will carry: three 50-pound bags of horse feed, a 50-pound trace mineral salt block, a large dead computer monitor, a new computer monitor in a large box, a trash bin, a box of 34 copies of my book, "Chivalry, Thy Name Is Bubba," and five bags of groceries.

The problem with the Matrix is that it insists that you wear a seat belt, even if you are, literally, a sack of potatoes. The groceries on the front seat weighed enough to trip the sensor in the car, and it began blinking and blaring, frantically trying to alert me to the life-threatening situation unfolding before its very LCD.

I asked the nice people at the dealership to unplug that feature, but they declined. So I'll have to get a shade-tree mechanic to do it, I guess.

You have to be careful how you do that, of course. One time we had a car with a security system in it. We didn't know that, because we had bought it used. It had a little light near the steering wheel that seemed always to be lit, but we didn't know what it meant. One time I left the door ajar overnight and the battery ran down. My husband, Cricket, hooked it up to a battery charger and, after a few hours, it revived. However, when it revived, the security system was activated and the car began emitting loud beeps, squawks and siren noises. We couldn't figure out how to turn it off, so Cricket finally just cut the wire.

Then, of course, the car thought it had been assaulted by a lawless pervert, and the engine wouldn't start.

My father had a similar experience at a most inopportune time.

My mother used to be involved in politics and from time to time she was invited to soirées at the White House. Daddy, who frequently complained about how much time she spent on politics, nevertheless found time on his own calendar to escort her to see the president. On one such occasion they were running a little late, and Daddy drove up to the guard box at the gate just as the other guests were walking in.

"We're with them," he said.

It's hard to imagine in this post-9/11 world, but the guard said, "Just pull on around and park by the rose garden."

So Daddy drove his big Lincoln around back.

They had a lovely time at the party. Gerald Ford was president then, and Daddy put the president at ease by telling him a joke. Momma had her picture taken with the president, but Daddy charmed the first lady by insisting on having his picture taken with her. As they were leaving, one of the guests asked Momma and Daddy for a ride. They went out to the rose garden, and all three got in the front seat of the car, laughing about their delightful evening. Daddy turned the key and nothing happened.

The three of them sat there for a minute contemplating the embarrassment of being stuck in the backyard of the White House with a dead battery. Finally, Daddy said, "I guess I'll have to go ask Jerry for some jumper cables."

At that point, the guest said she'd just walk back to the hotel, and she got out. Miraculously, as soon as she left, the car started perfectly.

As it turned out, the car had a safety feature that prevented it from starting unless the seatbelts were hooked. Daddy, who didn't like the idea of Detroit telling him when to buckle his seatbelt, had asked my brother to disconnect the wires. Cris had done so, but he figured they'd never have three people up front and he hadn't bothered to disconnect the wires for the middle seat.

Fortunately, the problem was resolved before Daddy had to go wake up the president.

CHAPTER 48

Is there such a thing as Type B?

Periodically I develop some troublesome physical problem that gradually becomes more and more aggravating, until finally I get scared and seek medical help. By the time I get to the doctor's office, I'm convinced that my symptoms are those of an incurable and fatal condition.

I've been through swollen glands, stomach irritation, colic, rashes, nausea, nose bleeds, back and neck pains – you name it. In each case, the doctor listens carefully to my description of this life-threatening condition, the onset of symptoms, the crescendo of suffering and the sorry pass to which I have come to at last. He nods seriously and does an examination. He orders blood tests. And then he calls me into his office to give me the awful news.

"It's stress."

This is always the diagnosis, no matter what my symptoms, no matter what part of my body is afflicted.

One time I had a bilateral bunionectomy, and I'm sure the need to shave bone spurs off my feet was a product of stress. At least, that's what the doctor said. (That, and too many years of jogging around downtown in spike heels.)

I cannot refute the diagnosis of stress because I'm a Type A – make that double-A – personality.

The online Merriam-Webster Dictionary says a Type A personality "is marked by impatience, aggressiveness, and competitiveness and … is held to be associated with increased risk of cardiovascular disease."

Having the drive of a Type A personality is helpful if you are a reporter, which I used to be, in an earlier life. But now I am seeking balance in my life and a transformation to a serene, Type B personality. It is not going well.

According to a 1998 paper titled "Transforming Type A Personality" by Carol H. Lankton, M. A., LMFT, "A truism for most Type A personalities is that it is much better to burn out than fade away."

Burnout I'm very familiar with. The pain of burnout is such that whenever I am hit with the consequences of my self-inflicted stress, I make a brave but short-lived attempt to transform my personality. Transforming the Type A personality is, I would say to Ms. Lankton, an oxymoron, a quixotic quest.

Recently, I have been to see several medical professionals about the pain in my neck. Some of my work with the Virginia Racing Commission had become a pain in the neck, literally and figuratively, so I resigned, but after several months, my neck pain was worse. My neck was frozen at the angle necessary to hold on my shoulder a telephone with which I had been conducting world affairs while simultaneously typing newspaper columns, folding laundry, washing the dog, cleaning the barn, transplanting azaleas, etc.

Relaxing my petrified neck cords was a challenge. In addition to muscle relaxants, the doctor prescribed neck exercises. I took the booklet home and read faithfully the procedures for performing various exercises. (This is harder than it looks.)

Before long, I found myself vigorously "rowing a boat" and rolling my head around on my shoulders like a hammer thrower winding up for the throw. Then I took two of the exercises and combined them, in the name of efficiency and getting well faster. I drove myself to get over being stressed as quickly as possible.

Finally, it dawned on me that maybe exercising my neck obsessively and compulsively wasn't what was called for. Sure enough, the booklet said, These are relaxing exercises.

Oh. I get it. You're supposed to stop what you're doing – no multi-tasking – and give yourself over to the exercise. It's not a contest with yourself to see how fast you can do the set, or how many reps you can do each day.

But relaxing is not as easy as it sounds.

I've been getting a massage now and then to work the tension out of my frozen neck muscles. The massage therapist is a kind, soft-spoken, soothing person who lights candles and plays rain-forest music to lull you into a sort of half-sleep. But, to the therapist's consternation, I'm always talking to her. Plus, I like to look at people when I'm talking to them, so I twist around to face her, forcing her to interrupt her soporific strokes.

"So, how long have you been doing this?"

"How many massages can you handle a day?"

"Is this a good place to work?"

"How did you get interested in this? Where did you get your training? Don't you have to have really strong arms? What do you do when you get sore? Does somebody give you a massage?"

The reporter in me will not die, or even go to sleep.

And it's starting to stress me out.

CHAPTER 49

The Epic Voyage of "*My Passion*"

Even though I am deathly afraid of driving off a bridge and drowning in a car, I have long been enamoured with sea stories and books about the water. Nautical memoirs such as Jack London's "The Cruise of the Snark" and Thor Heyerdahl's "Kon-Tiki," William Warner's biography of the Chesapeake Bay, "Beautiful Swimmers," and Joshua Slocum's classic "Sailing Alone Around the World" all hold an honored and inspirational place in my mind. Being on the water for an extended period of time invigorates the intellect and loosens the juices that have become turgid and thick in the rigid grid of routine. A boat sets a man free as the lines on the grid melt away and he sails over his life like a seagull.

I was thrilled and a little apprehensive, then, when the opportunity to make an historic voyage came to me. While romantic in prospect, the trip held enough comforting realism to draw me onboard.

The voyage was to be a shakedown cruise of *My Passion*, a 43-foot Hatteras sedan cruiser that the Captain had enjoyed dockside but had not sailed anywhere much. The planned itinerary would cover a week and two states and would at no time put the boat beyond access to hygenic personal comforts – or so we thought.

Most of my favorite men in the world would comprise the crew: my daddy, my uncle and my two brothers. Only my husband, Cricket, was missing. He felt one of us should stay home and make a living. The decision was comforting to me in that our child would not be left an orphan should the boat prove unseaworthy.

Another comfort was the assurance that we would not actually sail out into the Atlantic Ocean. The trip would be confined to manmade canals linking various natural bodies of water in a continuous path known formally as the Intracoastal Waterway, also known as The Ditch. Along with my car-off-the-bridge worries, I have a general fear of being too far out in the ocean to swim back to shore in the event of some boat malfunction. My fears along that line are not as severe as my mother's. She has often said of the early European explorers and settlers, "If had been up to me, we'd all still be in England." Nevertheless, I see no need to court danger by venturing further from shore than, say, the length of a good extension cord.

Over the years, the Captain – my daddy – bought and sold a number of boats in the 42'-48' range, generally keeping them tethered to a dock in Urbanna, Va., just off the Rappahannock River. Once he became comfortable motoring out to Buoy 6 and back, he began taking trips up and down the Inland Waterway, occasionally leaving the boat down south somewhere for the winter, usually in South Carolina, his native state. In later years, he kept his boat at the Norfolk (Va.) Yacht and Country Club, a day's sail closer to any southern destination.

My parents and their sailing guests told delightful stories of these trips, inspiring me one summer to leave my husband and baby for a week on the water myself. The voyage enabled me to experience the out-of-school rush that occurs when the lines are cast off and one's mind is loosened. The most dependable aspect of a boat trip is that the unexpected becomes the norm. Perhaps that is why cruising on the water frees up such profound human characteristics as courage, ingenuity and humor – and a certain preoccupation with basic human comforts. All of which inspired me to pen my own nautical memoir.

The Tour de Toilette

...being a guide to the water closets of the waterways of North Carolina, containing the personal reminiscences of the participants in a week-long boat trip, including good food, witty comments, boon companions and, of course, plenty of (clean) bathroom humor.

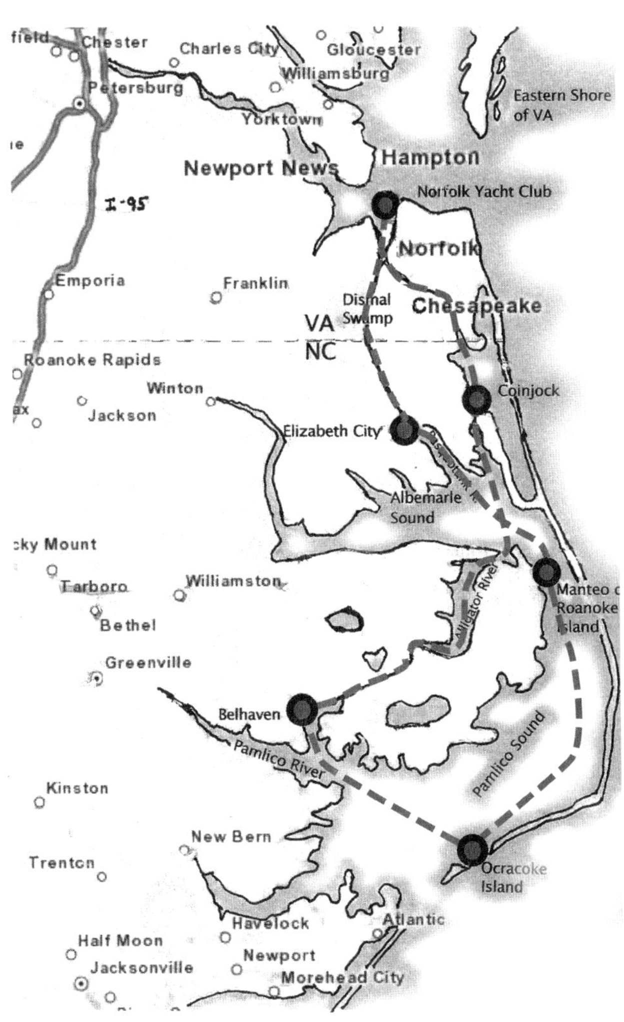

The investigatory team:

Daddy – The Captain
Uncle Dick – The Old Salt
My brother Bo – The Head Man (and Navigator)
My brother Cris – The Chief Engineer
And of course, Your Faithful Scribe

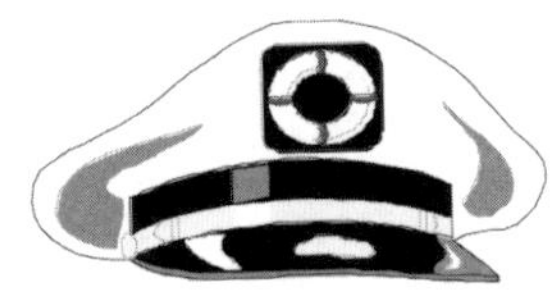

Day One
Thursday, June 19, 1997
Departure from Norfolk Yacht and Country Club, Norfolk, Va.
Destination: Midway Marina, Coinjock, N.C.

On a suitably hot summer day, the crew of *My Passion* assembled at the Norfolk Yacht and Country Club to begin a morning of sailing preparations, followed by an afternoon of trying to get the port engine to crank.

A 43-foot Hatteras with twin diesel engines, the good ship *My Passion* had previously been known by the somewhat suggestive name of *Passion*. The accommodations on board included a comfortable stateroom in the stern with two bunks, where the Captain and the Old Salt would toss their sea bags, and a pair of "V" berths in the bow, where my younger brother and I would camp, leaving the banquette in the saloon (that's boat talk for the couch in the living room) for my older brother to sleep on. Additionally, the boat had not one, but two heads -- with shower facilities! The galley boasted a real refrigerator and a three-burner range, but the Captain promised not to make me do all the cooking, even though I didn't know how to do anything else on the boat.

The Captain had taken *My Passion* on sea trials of an hour or so, out to

Buoy 6 and back, but this was to be the shakedown cruise of the vessel: a weeklong voyage south along the Inland Waterway, across Pamlico Sound to Okracoke Island, N.C. and back north through Elizabeth City and the Dismal Swamp Canal.

The first thing that happened was the port engine wouldn't start. When Your Faithful Scribe arrived, Bo and Cris had opened the hatch and gone down into the engine compartment, where they were to spend a good portion of the coming week. The brothers were armed with a hammer to perform delicate adjustments to the starter. As Cris applied the hammer in a precise manner, he told the Captain to keep hitting the starter for the port engine. After two hours of fruitless tapping, the Captain said, "We might have to sit here all week and go 'bdn, bdn, bdn.'"

But we were spared that fate when, eventually, the delicate adjustments worked and the engine fired.

The Captain was so eager to get going, at last, that he shifted into gear and shot out of the slip at a high rate of speed. I thought we were going to smash through the opposite dock, which was full of boats, but in a move reminiscent of Sean Connery's gutsy call in "The Hunt for Red October," the Captain spun the wheel just in time to keep us from being dashed on the docks, although we rocked a few boats with our wake.

We cruised through Hampton Roads, admiring the U.S. Navy fleet – aircraft carriers, enormous even from a distance, and submarines under repair in dry dock, covered by tarps to discourage satellite spies, or perhaps simply for shade on a brutally hot day. On the Portsmouth side of the channel, we passed the dry dock where the ironclad warship CSS Virginia was built on the hull of the USS Merrimac, leading to the first battle of ironclad warships in 1862 and ending the wooden navy. The difficulties with *My Passion*'s port engine had disrupted our schedule, so, further along, we idled near the U. S. Navy's "mothball fleet" of decommissioned ships as we waited for some drawbridge to open. Sliding under the enormous bow of the battleship *Wisconsin*, moored in a row of ships that saw ferocious action in World War II, Korea, even the Gulf War, we held a spontaneous moment of reverent silence.

In Virginia, history is everywhere you look.

On down the Elizabeth River below Norfolk, we went through the Great Bridge Locks and stopped on the far side for fuel, sidling up to a long concrete wall with huge pilings embedded at intervals. Although Daddy had had *My Passion* for almost a year, he had never bought any fuel. Consequently, he didn't know where the fuel tank cap was. So when the dockmaster came along with the fuel hose and said, "Where do you take on fuel, Cap'n?", Daddy looked around vaguely and said, "Your guess is as good as mine."

The dockmaster looked annoyed but refrained from cursing out loud at this smart aleck. He just said, "Here's the hose. I've got another customer." So Your Faithful Scribe read the boat manual while the men searched the decks and looked under the cabin carpet for the fuel cap.

With full fuel tanks, we motored ahead to our evening's destination, Coinjock, a tiny village known mainly for being the intersection of two major transportation arteries: the Inland Waterway and Route 168, the highway to the vacation Mecca of the Outer Banks.

The dock at Midway Marina, as at Great Bridge, is a long bulkhead along the main channel. As we idled off the dock, the dockmaster told us the current was running south and we might want to turn around and dock facing north. Then he told us about the electrical hookups on the port side and so on.

I paid careful attention to the latter information, since my task during docking was to hand the electrical hookup to Cris. But the dockmaster confused me. I couldn't understand what difference it made whether we plugged in on the left or the right side. I thought the gist of the dockmaster's instructions was: the *electrical* current was running a different direction because we were in North Carolina. I was relieved to find the power in North Carolina worked the same as in Virginia.

While at Coinjock, I took some pictures of Sue, the proprietor's daughter, who cheerfully waves to all the passing vessels. Among the regularly passing vessels is the tugboat *Sture*, skippered by my brother Bo. Bo is taking a busman's holiday by crewing *My Passion*, but he would never miss a chance to hang out with the family, even if it means driving the same route he drives the rest of the month.

Bo's engineer on the *Sture*, who is about 60, has a crush on Sue. He's never met her, of course, because the tugboat never stops. But, having loved her from afar for months, he has proposed tying a love note to a potato and throwing it across to the dock as they pass. So we have all come to refer to Sue, whose name was previously unknown, as "the potato girl." Pictures of the potato girl were subsequently posted on the *Sture*.

Everyone has been recounting adventures of past boat trips. The Captain has brought two boats up from Florida, *Sun Dog* and *Bateau*. He has taken a boat south to Hilton Head for the winter four times.

On one such trip, they tied up at the Beaufort (S.C.) Municipal Dock on Thanksgiving Day and called the Captain's sister, Aunt Bruce. The cousins were having dinner and someone drove to the dock and picked them up so they could have Thanksgiving dinner, too.

Another time, the Captain and his bride and some friends were going down this very waterway and they missed the Fairfield Bridge opening. The bridge wasn't scheduled to open again until the next day, so they tied up in an old canal nearby and had Thanksgiving dinner on the boat.

My brothers and I paid deference to Uncle Dick, who has more years of boating experience than all of us put together, by calling him the Old Salt. When his turn to tell a story came, the Old Salt recalled a time he and his bride tied up at Coinjock in high weather with a bunch of other boats. Finally, after three days, a European sailor on a 70-foot Viking power yacht decided to have a go at it. The Old Salt asked him to radio back when he got to wide open Albemarle Sound and let the others know how it was. The boaters tied up at Coinjock waited anxiously until they heard his distinctive accent crackling on the radio: "Tell the leetle boats not to go on!"

Another time, the Old Salt and his bride were cruising in Florida on a very nice 38-foot sailboat that they were proud of. They radioed ahead to a marina to reserve a slip for the night. The marina operator warned that they were very busy, very full, but after going on a bit, she said, "How long is your boat?" So Uncle Dick said 40 feet, and she laughed and said, "Oh come on. We can put that little boat somewhere."

The Midway Marina at Coinjock seems to be the Coinjock Country Club. Groups of young people hung around the café tables by the dock throughout the afternoon and evening. At one point, Uncle Dick, a man of gentlemanly leanings, said in surprise, "She's showing her butt!"

We all looked, and there was a girl in her 20s dropping trou to show her friends (male and female) – and the crew of *My Passion* – the tattoo on her rear end. I expressed surprise that she would pull her pants down so publicly, but Cris said anyone who had a tattoo was not likely to be of such delicate sensibilities as to be modest about revealing it, regardless of the location.

So I said, "You mean 'modesty' and 'having a tattoo' are an oxymoron…"

"…with the accent on moron," said Cris.

Although some of us later became more tactful about tattoos as our children acquired them, we were in agreement that day about the undesirability of body art. We were also in agreement about the quality of the bathhouse facilities at Midway Marina, which were clean, modern and – in a feature we came to appreciate later in the trip – open all night.

Day Two
Friday, June 20, 1997
Departure: Coinjock, N.C.
Destination: Dowrey Creek Marina, Bellehaven, N.C.

This morning the Chief Engineer gave the starter on the port engine a scientific tap with the hammer and the engine started with minimal delay. We enjoyed an hour or so of carefree cruising before the next mechanical issue arose.

In an ominous turn of events, the heads were not functioning correctly. This meant Uncle Dick and I had the deck to ourselves while the Captain, the Head Man and the Chief Sanitation Engineer spent a relaxing day rerouting the plumbing and commenting on the capabilities of a certain mechanic back in Norfolk.

Not that the others noticed, but today we came through the canal that connects the Alligator and Pungo rivers. It is a straight shot, maybe 20 miles long, with muddy water overhung on both sides by bushes and trees falling into the water. The bow of the boat cut a perfect "V" in the water and the long ripples of our wake splashed the bushy banks behind us. My normal shift in the skipper rotation fell during the canal transit, which meant I didn't get to turn the wheel more than an inch either way for the entire hour. Uncle Dick served as navigator, which involved standing at my elbow and comparing the straight line of the canal in front of us with the straight line of the canal on the chart. He explained that the canal was one of many shortcuts built to connect rivers and sounds along the East Coast, across Florida and along the Gulf Coast during World War II. The resulting inland waterway provided a protected north-south-southwest route for domestic shipping at a time when German U-boats were patrolling our coast and sinking hundreds of cargo vessels.

After awhile, Dick and I noticed something large and dark moving crossways in the canal way ahead. We thought it might be a log or an alligator, or maybe a big dog, possibly even a U-boat. Finally I took the glasses up on the bow while Dick took the wheel and, when the creature emerged from the water, I saw it was a large calf, maybe a yearling. An unexpected water hazard!

Meanwhile, Cris and Bo, in a good imitation of Ralph Cramblin and Norton, continued working on the sewerage system. It seemed the mechanic in Norfolk had hooked up various lines wrong, so the system worked but only under certain conditions conditions we seldom met, as it turned out. This was the same mechanic who had burned up the port engine starter and messed up a few other things, so Daddy said, "I'm through with him!"

Cris confided, "He doesn't read the instructions."

That evening we docked at a fairly new marina with clean, modern showers that also stayed open all night, a feature we appreciated in light of the malfunctioning heads onboard. Nevertheless, the highlight of the stay at Bellehaven remains to this day the people in the next boat.

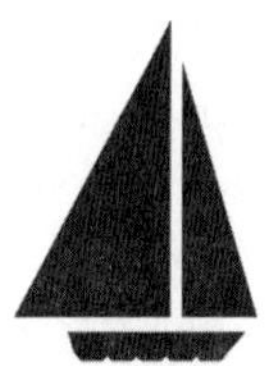

A sailboat pulled in across the dock from us, and we all noticed the occupants: a beer-gutted older man, a smaller man in purple trunks and a 50-ish woman with big knockers and an eentsy-teentsy bikini. We sniggered about them (the people, not the appendages) all evening. Well, some of us sniggered about the appendages. The Captain kept saying, "I was afraid she was going to lose one!" which prompted discussion of what the observer of such an event would do.

Since they were on a sailboat with an open cockpit, we had a good view of their docking procedure, cocktail hour and many other things. The woman, who was bleached blonde and had an accent unanimously estimated to be Swedish, was doing all the work: putting out bumpers and putting away cushions, fixing drinks, dumping ice, etc., prompting me to say, "Maybe she's their love slave, with the emphasis on slave."

Daddy opined she was with the beer-gutted older man "because he has the money."

We wondered if they had a ménage à trois. Bo, who had chosen to sleep on deck at night in the fresh air, said he was afraid the Swedish love slave would look across the dock and see him and come get him.

Yuk yuk yuk.

Eventually it occurred to us to wonder what they were saying about us: two older men, two younger men and one woman.

"She's their sister, right!"

"And that's her daddy and her uncle, sure!"

Day Three
Saturday, June 21, 1997
Departure: Bellehaven, N.C.
Destination: Anchorage Marina and Hotel, Okracoke Island, N.C.

The port engine started the first time today, without any hammer taps from the Chief Engineer or the Head Man. Bo and Cris joked about it, using all the touchy-feely terms of the day.

"The healing has begun," said Cris.

"We have closure on this," said Bo.

"You'd better not say that," I warned.

"Or we might get real closure," said Cris.

"As in shut down," I said.

The port engine ran fine, but there was a mysterious clunk in the starboard engine that caused some worry among the cognoscenti but not enough to shut it down.

We made a five-and-a-half hour run down the Pungo River, where we left the Inland Waterway and turned east down the wide Pamlico River, crossing the bottom of Pamlico Sound to Okracoke Island. Okracoke is a breakwater against the Atlantic Ocean, a long strip of barrier island with a wide place on the south end for a village. It is accessible only by ferryboat or private vessel. We tied up at Anchorage Marina and Hotel, where the Captain did a masterful job of docking that left the dockmaster truly impressed. The Captain had to more or less parallel park the boat after dodging several other vessels in tight quarters with the wind blowing about 15 knots.

We had the better part of the afternoon in port, so the Head Man, the Chief Engineer and Your Faithful Scribe set out to explore the island on bicycles.

First things first, of course: We investigated the head facilities, since they were still quite limited on board. The marina had a primitive, unisex bathroom with no shower; worse, it was available only by key from the dockmaster from 6 a.m. to 6 p.m. Exploring further, we went into the hotel office and Bo asked the desk clerk if there was a bathroom. She thought we were tourists and told us to use the ferryboat dock. Bo explained we were docked at the hotel's marina and we wanted to use the bathroom but the one at the marina was open only from 6 a.m. to 6 p.m. So the girl said, "What time do you want to use it?"

Which took us all aback and raised numerous questions.

"We were just planning ahead," said Bo, but we left wondering if we needed a reservation, or maybe even a credit card. Then we envisioned the girl taking reservations: name, address, phone, boat length, time of bathroom use… "Oh yes," mocked Bo, "the Traywicks, they're nine-o'clockers."

Then Cris quoted the American Express ad: "If you go to Okracoke, take your American Express, because they keep the bathroom locked and they don't take Visa."

We were getting a little silly from the salt air.

We rented bikes and rode around the island for several hours, visiting the lighthouse (for Cris), the ocean side of the island (for Bo) and the gift shop (for me). Unfortunately, the very first thing we did on the three-hour bike trip was to stop at a vegetable stand and buy tomatoes. They bounced around in the bike basket until we had catsup.

At the gift shop, Cris bought a coconut carved and painted as a pirate's head for his son and a horse t-shirt for his daughter. Bo bought t-shirts and a dried spiny blow-toad sprouting some serious spikes. I bought a pirate t-shirt and various fish, including a spiny blow-toad, with the idea of hanging them from the ceiling in a beach-themed bathroom back home (since bathrooms were on my mind).

Riding home with our purchases, Bo tried to sling the bag of tomatoes and the bag with the spiny blow-toad over his handlebars. The heavy bag of tomatoes knocked the spiny blow-toad into his bare leg, so then he carried one bag in each hand. In what is still one of the best memories among the three of us siblings, we roamed around the island for hours, laughing and enjoying being together on a sunny afternoon with no responsibility.

Back on the boat, we admired the other vessels in the harbor: a Chinese junk taking tourists for a sunset sail, a 72-foot Berger yacht with the shades drawn, concealing untold luxuries, and a 36-foot Bertram sport fisherman that Cris and Bo said they would take care of if my Bertram-loving husband would buy it.

After a fine dinner on board, the five of us walked around the harbor to the ferryboat dock. While we were there, we took the opportunity to inspect the public bathrooms. They are commodious and look like you would expect the public restrooms at a ferryboat dock to look. Still, they were open all night.

We spent the rest of the evening on deck watching a man at the outdoor bar on the dock cleaning fish with flair and dispatch, a one-man assembly line. He was fascinating to watch, and when we got up the next morning, he was still at it!

Day Four
Sunday, June 22, 1997
Departure: Okracoke Island, N.C.
Destination: Salty Dog Marina, Manteo, Roanoke Island, N.C.

We laughed about the (lack of) bathroom facilities at Okracoke – and our own desperation – the rest of the trip. Daddy said, "I went to the hotel this morning to check out and to see if they had any public restrooms… and I went in a door, and it was someone's room! This woman was getting dressed!"

Ever the wit, Cris said, "Did you ask if you could use her bathroom?"

That would have really fixed our wagon. The Anchorage Hotel people would be saying, "What is it with those people? Those perverts…"

We decided Jeff Foxworthy was the patron saint of the voyage. I bought his book, "No Shirt, No Shoes, No Problem," in Coinjock and Cris and I sat up giggling every night as I read him salient (and salacious) paragraphs. The Captain had to call us down one night!

Foxworthy is all about bathroom humor, which was appropriate.

Cris and I were bunking in the V-berths in the forward cabin because we are the two who get up, ahem, somewhat later than the others. We didn't want to make up our berths with sheets because that was too much trouble and hey, this was a vacation, but it was too hot to sleep in sleeping bags and modesty forbade the alternative. So we tinkered with the temperature in our quarters every night. He had brought a fan that we placed at the "V" of the V-berths and that we took turns kicking all night. Then we opened and shut the portholes, taking into account the mosquitoes, the prevailing wind and so on. One or two nights we got it right.

Coming up Pamlico Sound was rough today – windy, two-foot seas coming in from the stern quarter. Pamlico Sound is very big. We were out of sight of land for a long time and often out of sight of channel markers in the haze. As a professional tugboat captain in real life, the Head Man was also our Chief Navigator. He carefully plotted our course and channel markers dutifully appeared as he predicted. But at one point the Captain got anxious about seeing nothing but water all around and said, "I don't see any dove with an olive branch."

As we motored through the haze, Bo quoted one of his tugboat crewmen: "It's the poor disability (visibility) out there. I can't see the deacons (beacons)."

We laughed about "the deacons" several times and then Cris, who is a deacon in the Presbyterian Church, went up to the bow. I was at the wheel, so I told Bo, "I see a deacon up there."

The crossing was rough enough to make me queasy (admittedly, it doesn't take much), but I found that, as in the car, being at the wheel was a help. We had been changing who was at the wheel every hour on the hour, leaving the Head Man out of the rotation to attend to his duties as Chief Navigator. The Old Salt followed Your Faithful Scribe in the rotation and, as befits an old salt, he was ever ready to take the wheel at the first sign of weariness in Your Faithful Scribe. On this day, though, Your Green-faced Faithful Scribe clung to the wheel for every second of her appointed hour, beating off all attempts to relieve her.

The Captain's four days of relaxation came to naught this afternoon as we were coming into Manteo. The channel gradually narrows and it was chock full of crab pots. There was such a spread of them that Daddy had to dodge this way and that, with Bo beside him helping him find the channel markers and pick the crab pots out of the wavelets twinkling in the sun. It was a very stressful hour.

Once we got tied up at the Salty Dog Marina, Bo and I took the marina courtesy car and drove around, on the pretext of getting artichoke hearts for the salad I was making for dinner. We went around to a little waterfront commercial area we could see from the slip, and from there we discovered a bridge to an island where we found the Outer Banks Historical Center under construction. The construction was of no interest but parked alongside a dock beyond the unfinished building was the *Elizabeth II*, a replica of the ship that first came to Roanoke Island.

It being Sunday, everything was closed, but, nothing daunted, Bo and I jumped the turnstile and climbed two fences to get out to the ship. We crawled all over it. It measured 17 feet by 69 feet and weighed "50 tunnes" according to the sign. There were three levels below deck, counting the bilges. We marveled that people spent three months on board such a ship coming across the Atlantic.

And then, as Bo pointed out, they landed in a marsh with no food, no one to greet them, no shelter, no Wal-Mart. Seventeen by 69 feet – that would be like the 72-foot Berger we saw in Okracoke, only without the microwave.

We also found another 36-foot Bertram for Cricket.

While Bo and I were exploring Manteo, the Old Salt went out to dinner with his son, Dart, who lives nearby. Afterward they sat on board and visited awhile. It was great to see Dart, who was my best friend when we were in elementary school.

The Captain reminisced about the trip he and some friends made up the waterway with *Sun Dog*, a boat he bought Florida. They were in the slip fixing to leave one morning when they discovered the wheel would not turn. They nearly tore the helm station apart before they gave up and asked the mechanic at the marina to look at it. He came on board, glanced at the control panel and flipped a switch to turn off the auto-pilot – a feature no one knew the boat even had.

The facilities available for personal hygiene at the Salty Dog Marina were, we all agreed, the best of the trip, and the younger members of the crew enjoyed them thoroughly. The Captain and the Old Salt stuck to the shower on board.

Day Five
Monday, June 23, 1997
Departure: Manteo, N.C.
Destination: Pelican Marina, Elizabeth City, N.C.

We had a short run today, 8:30 a.m. to 2 p.m., but plenty of action. We zigged and zagged through crab pot markers going out of the channel and ran against the wind and rough water motoring up Albemarle Sound to the Pasquotank River. Once in the river, things smoothed out considerably.

No bike rides today. Cris and Bo spent the afternoon in the engine room again, this time trying to determine why the fuel in the port tank hadn't gone down but the fuel level in the starboard tank had.

On the bright side, they had worked on the starboard engine transmission that morning and had gotten the "clunk" out.

By the time this shakedown cruise is over, they joked, everything will be fixed, the boat will be perfect – and Daddy will sell it and look for another one!

Daddy said, "No, this is the last boat. I'm not going to get any more."

He was bombarded with jeers of "Fat chance!" and "Famous last words!" until he said, "Y'all are picking on me."

Editor's note: The crew was right. The Captain sold "My Passion" and subsequently bought half a dozen more boats, retiring from the water only after selling "Last Boat #5."

Part of every day was spent analyzing mechanical problems like this:

The port tank is full. The starboard tank is down. Is the port return pulling all the return to that tank? If we run long enough will it overflow? Should we cut off the starboard tank, run the engine and see if it's drawing from the port tank at all?

My contribution to this conundrum was: Fill up the starboard tank and keep going.

That was rejected as being too simple. So we ran the port engine for 20-30 minutes to see if it would cut off. If it did, that would mean the fuel was not coming from the port tank.

Dick posited that the overboard vent got clogged and created a vacuum so no fuel could get out.

Bo said during our rough crossing of Albemarle Sound, a piece of rust could have fallen off the inside of the tank and gotten sucked up against the intake screen, stopping the flow. Once we stopped and cut the engine off, it would have fallen away. In that case, everything would work fine now.

(When we were not discussing bathrooms, this is the sort of thing we would talk about.)

After 10 minutes of operating with the port tank open and the starboard tank closed, we saw the fuel gauge on the starboard engine creeping up. That meant fuel was returning to the starboard, as well as port, engines.

Cris said, "At this rate we'll never have to buy fuel."

Alas, the results of the test were inconclusive. Bo's theory was not ruled out. Other theories were presented. Perhaps there was some restriction in the return line of one tank? The good news was that we had a mechanical problem to mull over during any lull in the conversation about plumbing problems or interesting neighbors docked nearby.

And the Great Bathroom Tour continues…

After checking in with the dockmaster at Pelican Marina, Daddy returned with the news that the bathroom was locked…but there was a combination! We could use it after hours!

"The combination is 2-4-5-9," he said, "but first you have to push 'C' – for 'commode.'"

Not "C" for "clear."

We all fell out laughing.

Pelican Marina not only offers clean, accessible bath facilities, it has a well-stocked ship's store. The marina is centrally-located near the historic waterfront that is being renovated into upscale condominiums and fern bars. We took a break from pondering mechanical issues and walked up town where the Old Salt took us to dinner in a diner. The Colonial Restaurant was the last place in town with home-cooked food, the waitress said. Daddy, who spent a certain period of his life eating at diners and is therefore something of an expert, said, "I bet you can get good food here: it's full of local people and fat waitresses."

The food was good. We particularly enjoyed the fried grey trout.

After dinner, we retired to the deck of the boat for our customary post-prandial reminiscing. Working on the boat in a strange marina reminded us of the time in 1981 when the Captain decided to sail *Double Eagle* to Norfolk from what was then his home port on Urbanna Creek. The occasion was the wedding of Cris' friend, Lloyd Agnew. Momma and Daddy planned to stay on the boat all week at the Cavalier Yacht Club, site of the wedding reception.

It was a week of disaster that required the heroic and skilled efforts of both of the Captain's sons to keep *Double Eagle* off the bottom of the Elizabeth River. The trouble started during the trip down in a sou'easter when the rough water ripped off the spray rail. Then the marine police stopped them for speeding in Lynnhaven Inlet.

By the time they got to the Cavalier Yacht Club, the carpet in the cabin was floating, courtesy of leaks through the screw holes left empty when the spray rail ripped off. Daddy decided the leak wasn't too bad, and he just ran the bilge pump every so often to keep things under control. One night, though, he forgot to turn off the pump and burned up the motor. It was midnight, the club was closed and *Double Eagle* was sinking. Daddy ran up the dock and got the night watchman. They tried the dockmaster's pump and when that failed, they called the fire department to pump out the boat. Nobody in the marina got much sleep that night.

The next morning, Cris left work in Richmond and took a new bilge pump to Norfolk, 100 miles away. He and Daddy spent the day in the hold installing that, while Momma was entertaining guests aboard! The guest couple had brought their adult son, who was drinking all Daddy's beer and saying endearing things like, "Where's some more beer?"

According to Cris, Momma kept going down the companionway and hissing at Daddy: "Would you please get up here! I'm trying to entertain guests!"

To which Daddy would growl: "Well, I'm trying to keep the damn boat from sinking!"

They got things stabilized and Cris returned to his job in Richmond. The next day, Bo came down from Deltaville, 80 miles away, bringing some wooden pegs he had carved and dipped in lead paint. He went over the side and hammered them in the hull where the holes from the spray rail screws were letting the water come in.

Bo had brought his children with him. They were babies, so Momma took them to the beach to get them out of the way while Bo worked and Daddy waved his arms around. There was Momma on the beach with two babies with nothing to drink, no clean diapers and nothing to do with the dirty ones.

Cris came back down on Friday with Jill, his wife, to participate in the wedding festivities. They stayed on the boat, too. It was hot summertime, and Daddy had provided shade with a nice-looking but homemade canvas bimini erected over the deck on the stern. That night it rained and filled up the bimini. Sometime in the quiet of the night everything popped loose, and millions of gallons of water whooshed over the side and into the porthole beside Daddy's berth, where he was sleeping at the time.

Jill and Momma were sleeping in the V-berths in the forward cabin. The glass of the hatch above them had a skim of water sloshing around in it. When the bimini popped, it woke Jill up. She looked up and saw the water-filled hatch and almost cried because she thought the boat was under water.

After a fun-filled week of boat repairs in a strange marina, Momma and Daddy were still game enough to dress up and enjoy the wedding.

My husband, Cricket, and I went to Norfolk for the wedding, too, and we also stayed on the boat, once it had been certified as safely afloat. After the reception, Cricket wanted to run over to Virginia Beach and relive a certain carefree period of his youth. We tried several of his favorite bars, but it was hard to recapture the beachbum mood as we cozied up to the kids in flip-flops in our wedding finery. In desperation Cricket called his old running mates, only to find they were in bed asleep. Disillusioned, we headed back to the marina, but we couldn't remember how to get there. At one point, we were wandering around a very bad part of Norfolk late at night in a car with no gas and I had visions of "Bonfire of the Vanities."

Cricket and I made it back to the boat safely, and the next day we joined Momma and Daddy for the long boat ride back to home port in Urbanna. Daddy drove very slowly to protect the damaged spray rail!

When the Old Salt and the Captain turned in, Bo and I went up on the bow and listened to the water lapping against the hull of the boat.

It was a good night for looking at the stars. Bo and I have been looking at the constellations all week. He knows them all from years spent on the water; he even learned to navigate with a sextant, like the early explorers. I know a few constellations and I've learned a few more on this trip: Virgo, Boötes and Cygnus the Swan, which is really a pretty constellation, but it takes a dark night and a lot of sky to see it properly. Spending time on the bow of the boat with my big brother, looking at the stars and musing about the world and the place of Man in it, turned out to be one of many fond memories of the trip for me – just as fond as laughing about Jeff Foxworthy in the V-berths with my younger brother.

Day Six
Tuesday, June 24, 1997
Departure: Elizabeth City, N.C.
At the South Mills Locks, Dismal Swamp, N.C.

This morning we got up early (even me!) and left at 6 a.m. to make the 8:30 a.m. lock opening. We got here at 8. I asked Dick to take a picture of me with the sunrise for proof of this historic occurrence, but he said no one would be able to tell from the photo whether it was sunrise or sunset. What a waste!

Once I got over that disappointment, I enjoyed the lovely ride up the Pasquotank River, so still in places there are water lilies.

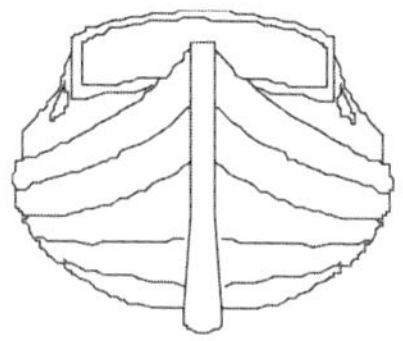

At South Mills Locks, we entered the Dismal Swamp Canal for a three-hour cruise home to the Old Dominion. Inside the towering walls of the locks, I took a childlike pleasure in watching the water pour in around us, lifting the boat to the level of the canal. The lock gates opened, slowly sweeping back the brown water to reveal the tree-hung channel stretching north to Virginia. The engine rumble, wind-blown in the expanse of Pamlico Sound, made the boat seem like a bellowing beast here in the tunnel of trees. We saw a muskrat swimming and a night heron and a kingfisher. I kept looking for snakes sunning on the branches over the canal but didn't see any. It was a snaky looking place, though. We did see a bear – dead, floating. We also saw some other dead things, bloated muskrats that looked like turkey carcasses.

The mayflies were so bad we had to shut the windows and zip the side curtains of the cabin cockpit, but within minutes it became stiflingly hot. Navigation was no issue in the canal, so crew members assisted the skipper by standing beside him and killing mayflies. It was a constant battle. Those devils would eat you up.

Later that same day
At the Deep Creek Locks, Dismal Swamp, Va.

I had the pleasure of being at the wheel as we approached the locks at the north end of the canal. The mayflies had abated somewhat, and

Daddy let me dock the boat to wait for the opening. This was a matter of pulling alongside the bulkhead, something that was possibly within my capabilities, as opposed to threading the boat through a pair of pilings into a slip. Daddy stood very close and told me what to do, of course, so I wouldn't tear up the bow on the concrete wall. It was pretty neat. I've watched him do it a lot, so I had an idea what to do. But it's not just a matter of knowing what you want the boat to do, it's more knowing how to work the transmission and throttle to get the boat to respond. Here at the end of the trip, it was exciting to learn how to do something on the boat besides boil coffee water. I can catch and throw lines, and I can steer, but my technical contribution to docking heretofore has been the ceremonial passing of the electrical connector to Cris.

We had to wait a couple of hours for the lock opening at the north end of the canal. You'd think they'd have that schedule coordinated better. Maybe it is timed for slow boats. Or maybe it is set up to support the local economy. There is a little Mexican restaurant right where we tied up. I stayed on the boat while the men went to get catfish sandwiches and fight over the check. As they hopped off the boat, I called to Cris and asked him to get me a quesadilla. Then Daddy and Uncle Dick wanted to know why I wanted a case of beer.

I guess you have to have a Southern accent to get that.

Going through the locks involved a dramatic drop of 10 or 12 feet, and it was hard to believe when the gates opened that the water on the other side would be at the same level. Definitely an eerie experience.

Still later that same day
Norfolk Yacht and Country Club, Norfolk, Va.

Because of the rush hour auto traffic, some drawbridges in Hampton

Roads don't open between 3:30 and 5 p.m., a fact that dictated our schedule from the time we left Elizabeth City at 6 a.m. We had to make the 1:30 p.m. lock opening at Deep Creek; anything later and we would spend the rest of the afternoon luffing around the Elizabeth River, looking at the U. S. Navy's mothball fleet, which we had already inspected thoroughly a week earlier.

But thanks to a well-executed itinerary, we hit all the bridge openings just right coming through Hampton Roads and made it from Deep Creek Locks to the slip in less than two hours.

We docked smoothly, tied up smartly and hosed down the boat. We said our farewells, proclaimed the trip a success, thanked the Captain and vowed to sail together again soon. Then we all went home. Home, where you can use the bathroom any time you want.

Just push "C" for "commode."

About the Author

My earliest memory is of finding a marble under a table in the living room. In the time-honored investigative method of a three-year-old, I put it in my mouth. It went down my windpipe, effectively blocking it. Fortunately, before too many nanoseconds passed, my survival instincts kicked in and I coughed the marble up.

Hmm, I thought, swallowing marbles is not a good thing.

I've been taking risks and learning from my experiences ever since.

I was reared in Lynchburg, Virginia and left in 1968 to attend Hollins University (née, Hollins College) where I met, for the first time, a Yankee. She had never met a Southerner. We both survived, unscathed. After many interesting experiences as a conservative during the height of the Sixties, the Vietnam War, the sexual revolution, the civil rights movement, the feminist liberation, Earth Day, flower power and other psychedelic scenes, I learned that I did not want to be anywhere near college or college students. So I dropped out and got married. Another learning experience.

Shortly thereafter I got divorced.

Over the ensuing years, I learned how to transfer from college to college without losing any credits, so that finally, seven years and five colleges after leaving Lynchburg, I got a degree. Two, in fact.

While transferring among colleges, I broke horses for the racetrack Virginia did not yet have and commuted from Virginia to Hawaii to attend some really great parties with friends in the U. S. Navy. While experiencing many wine coolers on the beach at Fort deRussey, I began writing The Great American Novel. After learning that writing a novel is not as easy as it looks, I returned to the mainland – and yet another college, with yet another major.

My all-time favorite "Doonesbury" cartoon comes from the early period, before the strip became a political diatribe, back when it was humorous. Zonker Harris is reminiscing about college and he says something like, "Ah, I remember being a sophomore. Three of the best years of my life." My thoughts exactly.

The University of Virginia was accepting girls by then and I went there long enough to revert to my old love – classical languages. I applied to UVA and UNC for graduate school in Latin and Greek, and you would not now be reading this but for a timely rescue by author Sylvia Wilkinson.

Sylvia was the writer-in-residence at Hollins in the spring of 1975, as I was closing in on a degree. We were at a party with the students in the graduate program in creative writing, and she asked if I were planning to attend the program the next year.

The conversation was more than a learning experience. It was a thunderbolt. Oh yeah, the reason I'm laboring through college is because I want to write.

Not teach Greek.

Thank you, Sylvia.

Following a wonderful year in graduate school under the incomparable Richard Dillard, I moved to Richmond with the expectation of getting a real job. At least, that was my parents' expectation, since I was 26 years old. Plus, I now had this horse to support, the offspring of the mare in foal that I had left on Daddy's doorstep during one of my longer commutes to Hawaii. The real job thing didn't pan out immediately, so I spent my late 20s as a Poor Starving Artist, typing – on a real typewriter – The Great American Novel while doing freelance writing and working at the Virginia General Assembly to support the horse.

This experience led me to the inescapable conclusion that I needed a real job or a successful husband. At the ripe old age of 30, I got both.

Cricket Williams rescued me from my artist's garret (and many other scrapes over the years).

Legendary editor Alf Goodykoontz got tired of my nagging him for a job at the Richmond Times-Dispatch and hired me as a feature writer. Thus began a +4-year period of many interesting experiences, among them a dispute with the judicial system about the meaning of "confidential sources".

After leaving the Times-Dispatch in 1984, I did a bunch of political stuff and some stuff with horses, but not nearly enough writing. There was a stint around 1989 when I wrote a weekly column for "The Goochland Free Press." And there was another stint about 1991 or –2 when I edited another weekly paper, "The Goochland Gazette."

Then about 1999, my mother nagged me into publishing a collection of my columns and other freelance work. The result was "Chivalry, Thy Name Is Bubba."

"That Bubba book" has been amazingly popular simply through word of mouth. It is especially popular as a holiday or birthday gift because the humor appeals to a wide audience. One of the articles appears as an excerpt in "Chicken Soup for the Horse Lover's Soul."

The publisher of the Chicken Soup books is Peter Vegso, and we got to be friends through horse racing. Eventually, a racetrack was built in Virginia, and I had the fascinating job of being on the Virginia Racing Commission, the regulatory agency that supervised the licensing, construction and operation of the track. Colonial Downs has the largest turf track in the country and hosts the Virginia Derby. Peter Vegso horses have won the Virginia Derby three times.

Ten years on the racing commission – six as chairman – gave me a terrific look at the most exciting sport in the world. Writers have always been fascinated by the racetrack, and I am not the first to try to capture the beauty, the pathos, the thrill and the intoxication of racing. I have been working on a racetrack novel for some time, and it is the most fun project I've ever written. I love my characters and part of me dreads the day their story will be finished – but another part of me is eager to share them with my readers.

In 2004, I resigned or retired from my political and racing activities in order to focus on writing. I am now working on two non-fiction book projects in addition to the racetrack novel. In the summer of 2005, I began writing a newspaper column under the title "Bush Hogs and Other Swine." The column appeared mostly in "The Goochland Courier," and thus I completed a hat trick by writing for three different weeklies in the same county.

In 2007, a racing-related project that I became involved in came to fruition: the establishment of a program at a nearby prison to provide rehabilitation and training in horse management to inmates, using rescued ex-racehorses. What I have learned from that amazing experience will certainly be the subject of a future book. Although it has cut into my writing time, my involvement with the Thoroughbred Retirement

Foundation, locally and nationally, has been one of the most personally rewarding experiences of my life. Since 2009, I have served as president of the national organization, which has provided me the opportunity to reconnect with many old friends in the racing industry. It has also given my husband and me an excuse to follow our daughter around as she blazes her own path in the racing industry.

All of these life experiences have led me to the realization that, while I have certain strong interests, I can't sit still and do one thing for long. After a spell of politics, I get itchy for horses; after horsing around, I get to hankering to write about all the characters I've dreamed up at the racetrack and on the campaign trail. It's about time now for me to rotate out of public life and back home to write, surrounded by my family and our animals, which is where I am happiest. In closing, then, I will quote a literary character of great profundity, Tigger: Ta ta for now.

September 2010

NOTES

NOTES

NOTES